WHAT MILLIONAIRE CEOS WILL NEVER TELL YOU ABOUT PRODUCTIVITY AND MOTIVATION

10 Productivity and Motivation Hacks You Need To Know To Be Successful In Business

BENJAMIN WALTERS

Copyright © 2018 by Evergreen Forest Publishing

No part of this publication may be reproduced, stored in a retrieval system, or transmitted in any form or by any means, electronic, mechanical, photocopying, recording, or otherwise, without written permission of the publisher.

Before We Start...

I would like to say thank you for purchasing this book. Without your support, this would have not been possible. So I would like to give you this **free** info graphics that will help you survive recession.

This info graphic will help you be prepared for the most significant financial crisis that everyone struggles from, and instead allow you to earn a massive amount of money during this time of chaos. Did you know there are hundreds of people who became millionaires because they were ready for the recession? Sounds entirely different than everyone else who went through the 2008 recession. But with this info graphics, I assure you that you can be one of those people.

SO WHAT ARE YOU WAITING FOR? CLICK ON THIS LINK TO TAKE ADVANTAGE OF THIS LIFETIME OPPORTUNITY AND REACH FINANCIAL FREEDOM.

https://tinyurl.com/recession-infographics

Disclaimer

This book is not intended to be replaced for your financial planner or advisor. I recorded all the things that have worked out for me, and I cannot guarantee that it will 100% work for you. This may or may not work in the future. I am not a professional investment advisor, and every investor should be aware that there are risks associated with investing and there could be a possibility that they could lose significant amount of money. I am not liable for any errors or omissions in the material or any losses that you may incur. By reading this, you consent to these statements. You are responsible for your due diligence and decisions.

Table of Contents

Before We Start...

    So what are you waiting for? Click on this Link to take advantage of this <u>lifetime opportunity</u> and <u>reach financial freedom</u>.

Disclaimer

Table of Contents

Chapter 1. To What Extent Does Labor Negatively Impact the Psychology of Humans?

    Introduction

    Correlation Between Economic and Psychological Welfare

    The Absence of Work

    Solutions and Limitations

    Works Cited

Chapter 2. The Toll of Long Work Hours

    Introduction

    Impact of Long Work Hours on Health

    Impact of Long Work Hours on Happiness

    Solution and Limitations

    Works Cited

Chapter 3. Automation: The Right Path Forward?

    Introduction

    Effectiveness of Automation

    Economic Impacts

Societal Implications

Solutions

Works Cited

Chapter 4. To What Extent Should Secondary Education Be Pursued?

Introduction

Debt and Money

Health Insurance and Pension Plans

Value of Degrees

Conclusion

Works Cited

Chapter 5. Using Creativity to Understand Western Political Health in the Past Half a Millenia: Do Paint Strokes Mirror Pen Strokes?

Introduction

The Government in Art

The Artist's Mind

Solution

Works Cited

Chapter 6. What are the Effects of Automation on Cultural Works?

Spare Time

An Assault on Repetition

Emotion and the Spread of Ideas

Conclusion: Cultural Niches with a Universal Cultural Platform

Works Cited

Chapter 7. Wage Inequality: To What Extent do the Wages of Executives Reflect Their Contribution to Society?

Introduction

Tricks of the Trade

Straight to the Source

Reap What You Sow:

Conclusion

Works Cited

Chapter 8. To What Extent Does Financial Incentives Affect Workers' Quality of Workforce?

Introduction

Worker's Expectation: The Implication of Being Rewarded Continuously

Limitation of Innovation: The Implication of Approved Method of Work

Recommendation

Works Cited

Chapter 9. Environmental Impact of Integrating Endangered Cultures into Modern Society

Works Cited

Chapter 10. Economic Impact of Endangered Culture Integration

Other Information and Implications

Works Cited

Other Books From Evergreen Forest Publishing

One Last Thing... .

This is the End...

So what are you waiting for? Click on this Link to take advantage of this lifetime opportunity and reach financial freedom.

Chapter 1. To What Extent Does Labor Negatively Impact the Psychology of Humans?

Introduction

Over the past few centuries, work has deeply integrated itself into human society and plays an essential role in the everyday lives of the majority of people. Labour is, by far, the most reliable way for one to support the needs of themselves and their families. Out of the estimated 322,225,731 people living in the United States of America on February 1, 2016 (U.S. and World Population Clock), approximately 123,474,000 people were employed in private industry (Employment change from the same month a year ago, in thousands, seasonally adjusted); over one-third of the population. The importance of labor in the United States is further suggested by the fact that in March 2016, 60% of the US population was between the ages of 18 and 65 (Population Distribution by Age) - the age group most frequently associated with employment. With all of this in mind, the implications of labor on all aspects of people's lives must be considered since work holds such a significant place in today's society, especially with regards to the psychological element. Psychology can be genetically defined as the science of mind and behavior (Definition of Psychology), and this keystone of human existence is pivotal to the successful function of society as a whole.

An important question to examine is to what extent the act of labor, both physical and intellectual, negatively influence one's psychology and the implications and limitations of potential solutions. Specifically, this paper focuses on the relationship between economic and psychological well-being, and psychology in the absence of work. In the article "A World Without Work," Derek Thompson argues that employment causes workers to develop a sense of guilt when they are not productive; that society has conditioned them to feel this way. It is also mentioned that work provides a sense of security and that workers feel "better and less anxious" while at their job. In this way, unproductivity, not work, negatively impacts worker's mental states, though work is, indirectly, the source of this guilt. As a result, labor itself negatively affects the psychology of humans to a limited extent. Ultimately, this paper argues that the United States government should provide legislation to guarantee paid vacation days based on the dissatisfaction of personal productivity being psychologically detrimental.

Correlation Between Economic and Psychological Welfare

Employment allows workers to gain compensation for their labor and support themselves financially, but without sufficient reimbursement, breakdown begins to occur in other areas of life. If someone is not adequately well-off economically, the psychological aspect of their lives may become strained. A study published by the American Public Health Association found that parents who relocated outside of high-poverty residential neighborhoods had the superior mental health to those who remained, apparent through their lower distress and depressive symptoms (Leventhal, Brooks-Gunn). The results of the study emphasize the profound correlation and connection between financial and psychological well-being, suggesting that a lack of economic prosperity does, in fact, cause hardships in other areas of life. Adam Smith takes a similar stance in Chapter X, Part 1, from "The Wealth of Nations." He contends that "the chance of gain is naturally over-valued"; in other words, people have exaggerated expectations that good fortune will come their way, and that they have an excessive belief in their abilities. Smith also asserts that the competitive nature of professions means not everyone will find considerable success in their job choice. High expectations combined with not reaching those expectations is a recipe for intense disappointment. A parallel to labor can be seen in elite varsity swimming in Canada. A study published by the Clinical Journal of Sports Medicine found that 66% of the elite top 25% of athletes assessed met diagnostic criteria for a major depressive episode, with 41% of the same group of swimmers reporting that they experienced mild to moderate symptoms of depression. This depression was found to be directly correlated with one's swimming performance based on their rank. Furthermore, in the sample of the top 25% athletes, the study ascertained that changes in swimming performance were significantly related to their current depression, but not their history of depression (Hammond et al.).

Since employment is a fundamental way to make income in modern society, it seems plausible that it would not cause psychological destitution using a salary that allows them to support themselves adequately. However, the affluent and successful do not necessarily have a superior mental state. In their book Culture and Subjective Well-being, psychologists Ed Diener and Eunkook M. Suh suggest that the accumulation of wealth has the potential to distract humans from focussing on their well-being and that the pursuit of this is mostly unfulfilling when it comes to satisfaction (Diener, Suh). Whatever one's salary may be, labor and associated wealth do not guarantee to be beneficial to one's psychology. It all comes down to the feeling experienced when time outside of the sanctity of work is wasted. Productivity primarily determines the extent to which one's psychology is negatively impacted.

THE ABSENCE OF WORK

Aside from the economic aspect of work, it provides a sense of purpose and meaning in many people's lives. Derek Thompson claims that people, for the most part, rely on their work to feel a lasting sense of purpose (Thompson). He professes that without steady employment, it would be difficult to fill the "vacuum of accomplishment" with leisurely activities. This raises two critical questions: how and to what extent does the absence of work negatively affect the psychology of humans, and how does this relate to the impact of labor itself?

A clear example of the negative influence of unemployment on psychology is in the American town of Youngstown, as detailed by Derek Thompson.

Approximately 50,000 jobs were lost when the town's steel mills closed down. A social, cultural, and psychological breakdown was a direct result of the unavailability of employment, which is apparent in the fact that "the caseload of the area's mental-health center tripled within a decade" (Thompson). In this case, it is not labor itself, but the lack thereof, that causes major psychological issues. This is primarily because of the problems that arise in the absence of work. Within the American structure of wealth distribution, unwanted joblessness means no source of income for individuals. People need a certain amount of money for food, rent, clothing, etc. depending on their chosen lifestyle, and some accumulation of wealth to support it. A survey-based study published in the Journal of Organizational Behavior found that increased social alienation is directly correlated with unemployment status (Winefield et al.). The fact that unemployment often causes social issues is another way that unemployment is psychologically harmful. According to neuroscientist John Cacioppo, loneliness causes hormonal stress, immune function issues, and a score of potentially harmful health problems (Shute). This further shows how unemployment is closely connected to detrimental psychology. Derek Thompson also mentions this concept. According to public-health professor Ralph Catalano, "There is a loss of status, general malaise and demoralization, which appears somatically or psychologically or both." He claims that since people do not have "a routine, an absorbing distraction, a daily purpose," it is highly challenging to cope with and recover from unemployment (Thompson).

This lack of self-purpose leads many to isolate themselves physically, socially, and psychologically.

Say, for example, an unemployed individual had enough money to support themselves. What would the average person do in their spare time? There is no better and broader example than that of retirees in America. According to a study published by the United States Bureau of Labor Statistics, when it comes to the spare time of the elderly, whether or not they were employed as a more critical factor than their age. The study found that unemployed men between the ages of 65 and 69 spent approximately 4.6 hours, on average, watching television, with similar disproportionately significant amounts of time spent watching TV in other age groups (Krantz-Kent, Stewart). Instead of being productive and devoting themselves to self-improvement, unemployed seniors tend to lean towards television as a staple leisure activity. This mainstream way to spend time leads to increased social isolation, even though they have decisively more time to dedicate to interacting socially with others. A likely cause of this goes back to Derek Thompson's point on how society has conditioned individuals to feel guilty when downtime is spent in an unproductive fashion (Thompson). For many, work is a reliable means to maintain a sense of purpose, since life can lose meaning if people feel dispirited at the way they spend their lives.

SOLUTIONS AND LIMITATIONS

Moving forward, how should American society adjust labor so that psychologically disturbing aspects of work are minimized? The workforce should be amended to encourage leisure as a means of psychological recuperation. American culture is mostly workaholic, with millions of laborers feeling so guilty about taking a paid vacation that they pass up the opportunity. 41% of American workers do not use all, or in some cases, any of their paid vacation days and 15% of senior managers feel that workers who utilize their paid vacation time are less dedicated to their work (Pinsker). They also believe that as a result of vacation time, they will fall behind in their job. American workers should be prompted to appreciate the personal psychological value of time off work. This would significantly diminish the psychologically undesirable guilt experienced while being unproductive - the main culprit when it comes to labor negatively impacting the psychology of humans. Because of all this, the culture surrounding leisure time in America needs to be modified.

    One implication of this would be the effects of increased leisure usage of employees in the workplace. A survey conducted by the Society for Human Resource Management, in collaboration with the United States Travel Association, found that the majority of human resources professionals contend that employee vacations make a "positive impact on performance, morale, wellness, culture, productivity, and retention" (SHRM/U.S. Travel Association: Vacation's Impact on the Workplace). These attributes are invaluable to productivity in the workplace, and despite not contributing to employment while on paid vacation, this loss of time is made up for by better work. According to a report by the Center for Economic and Policy Research, one-quarter of US workers are not allotted any paid vacation, because the United States does not require employers to provide paid vacation or holidays (Ray, Schmitt). The fact that the US government is the only advanced economy that does not guarantee paid leave for workers highlights that legislation is necessary for this area to ensure everyone has this right.

A limitation of this argument as a whole is that encouraging leisure time does not mean that workers and employers alike are sure to embrace it. Government regulations and legislation cannot change the attitudes of managers that using all of one's paid vacation is an irrefutable sign of a lack of commitment and devotion to their work. Likewise, laborers may continue to view leisure as purely unproductive, even without pressure from those above them in the workforce. Although legislation cannot indefinitely solve these problems in American society, it is an excellent place to start.

Altogether, this issue must be tackled with great urgency and efficiency. We must construct and implement government legislation to minimize the negative consequences of a workaholic American way of life.

Works Cited

"Definition of Psychology." *Merriam-Webster Dictionary*. Web,

> www.merriam-webster.com/dictionary/psychology. Accessed March 26, 2017.

Diener, Ed, and Eunkook M. Suh. "Culture and Subjective Well-being." *MIT Press*. eBook,

> books.google.ca/books?hl=en&lr=&id=1A2siA19h KYC&oi=fnd&pg=PA185&dq=money+and+happi ness&ots=2osr7e5_mr&sig=yt7qFesm-d9mjvWc86EovTsqCoo#v=onepage&q=money%2 0and%20happiness&f=false. Accessed April 8, 2017.

"Employment change from same month a year ago, in thousands, seasonally adjusted." *United*

> *States Bureau of Labor Statistics*. Web, www.bls.gov/web/empsit/tab4.txt. Accessed

March 26, 2017.

Hammond, Thomas, et al. "The Prevalence of Failure-Based Depression Among Elite Athletes."

> *Clinical Journal of Sport Medicine*, Jul 2013. Web,

> www.researchgate.net/publication/236080582_The _Prevalence_of_Failure-
> Based_Depression_Among_Elite_Athletes. Accessed April 1, 2017.

Krantz-Kent, Rachel, and Jay Stewart. "How do older Americans spend their time?" *United*

States Bureau of Labor Statistics, May 2007. Web,

www.bls.gov/opub/mlr/2007/05/art2full.pdf. Accessed April 8, 2017.

Leventhal, Tama, and Jeanne Brooks-Gunn. "Moving to Opportunity: an Experimental Study of

Neighborhood Effects on Mental Health." *American Public Health Association*, Sep

2002. Web, ajph.aphapublications.org/doi/full/10.2105/AJPH.93.9.1576. Accessed

March 27, 2017.

Pinsker, Joe. "41% of American Workers Let Paid Vacation Days Go to Waste." *The Atlantic*,

Aug 2014. Web,

www.theatlantic.com/business/archive/2014/08/41-percent-of-american-workers-let-their

-paid-vacation-go-to-waste/378950/. Accessed April 8, 2017.

"Population Distribution By Age." *The Henry J. Kaiser Family Foundation*. Web,

kff.org/other/state-indicator/distribution-by-age/?currentTimeframe=0&sortModel%7B%

22colId%22:%22Location%22,%22sort%22:%22asc%22%7D. Accessed March 26,

2017.

Ray, Rebecca, and John Schmitt. "No-Vacation Nation." *Center for Economic and Policy*

Research, May 2007. Web, cepr.net/publications/reports/no-vacation-nation. Accessed

April 8, 2017.

"SHRM/U.S. Travel Association: Vacation's Impact on the Workplace." *Society for Human*

Resource Management, Nov 2013. Web,

www.shrm.org/hr-today/trends-and-forecasting/research-and-surveys/pages/shrm-us-trav

el-vacation-benefits.aspx. Accessed April 8, 2017.

Shute, Nancy. "Why Loneliness Is Bad for Your Health." *U.S. News - Health*. Web,

health.usnews.com/health-news/family-health/brain-and-behavior/articles/2008/11/12/wh

y-loneliness-is-bad-for-your-health. Accessed April 8, 2017.

Smith, Adam. "Chapter 10, Part 1 from *The Wealth of Nations*." *AP® Capstone Program -*

Stimulus Materials, published Mar 1776. Web,

apcontent.collegeboard.org/sites/default/files/Seminar_PT2_2016-17_revised.pdf.

Accessed April 1, 2017.

Thompson, Derek. "A World Without Work." *AP® Capstone Program - Stimulus Materials*,

published Jul/Aug 2015. Web,

apcontent.collegeboard.org/sites/default/files/Seminar_PT2_2016-17_revised.pdf.

Accessed March 29, 2017.

"U.S. and World Population Clock." *United States Census Bureau*. Web,

www.census.gov/popclock/. Accessed March 26, 2017.

Winefield, A. H., et al. "Social alienation and employment status in young adults." *Wiley Online Library*. Web, onlinelibrary.wiley.com/doi/10.1002/job.4030120206/abstract. Accessed April 8, 2017.

Chapter 2. The Toll of Long Work Hours

Introduction

Today, our careers and work are an essential cornerstone of our lives. This is because work provides a means to live and ideally a source of expression. Some estimate that people will spend 30% of their time on Earth working, a sobering amount of one's life (Dalton). No doubt standard 40 hour work weeks feel like a long-standing practice, but working the current 9 to 5 is new to society. In previous centuries people worked six-day weeks, only in the early 1900s did Henry Ford introduced taking the weekend off to improve the well-being of his employees ("Who Invented Weekends?"). Similarly, it took the World Wars sweeping through Europe to enable women to work outside of their domestic roles ("The impact of WWII on women's work"). Working more jobs and more extended hours ended up trailblazing for modern feminism, allowing society to improve gender equality. The impact even touched western culture, such as Rosie the Riveter (Miller). Also, work in the future could even further change, potentially becoming obsolete, due to improving automation (Thompson 1). Furthermore, an aspect of work that is changing right now is that people are working significantly more than in previous decades, with 70% of people working overtime (Jarvis).

These particular shifts in society hold the common theme of work hours driving change. The changes in our workforce resulting from more extended work hours is essential. The average physical health and happiness are some of the defining aspects of society, and the lengthening work hours are closely tied to them. It is therefore essential to consider the result of long work hours on one's overall wellbeing. There is a spotlight on the fact that one's welfare is profoundly negatively impacted by excessive work hours. This raises the question of to what extent do long work hours adversely affect one's physical health and happiness, and how to negate it.

IMPACT OF LONG WORK HOURS ON HEALTH

A critical aspect to situate the impact of long work hours on one's well-being is how it affects one's health. No doubt, a lot of the ramifications happen indirectly from working long hours. There could be high amounts of stress involved which itself leads to health complications. And, depressingly, stress is only the start; long work hours also magnifies job-related risks due to the more prolonged exposure to them (Dembe 3). Furthermore, working long hours takes time away from the allotted 24 hours a day that a worker could utilize to take care of themselves. Employers stand to lose too when their employees work long hours, surprisingly.

First, working more extended hours leads to health complications from the stress. A study done by researchers at the Institute of Health in Japan showed that extensive work hours lead to arteriosclerotic diseases and heart attacks in middle-aged workers, all "triggered by long working hours" (Uehat 147). The workers did not just wake up ill though; they built up stress from their job for long enough that it led to health complications. This brings to light a symptom of Japanese society, where people devalue their personal needs to work longer, resulting in cases where they diminish their own well being and health (Nandi 2). It is unfortunate but the workaholic aspect of the Japanese arose from terrible hardships in the World Wars, so it is understandable. Regardless the outcome of this results in the deterioration of the health of the Japanese workforce.

Ultimately, a feedback loop results from work-related stress. The additional work takes time away from what they could spend taking care of themselves, leading to a worse performance in their job. A way that this could surface would be lost sleep. A study done over the course of 20 years with 52000 participants found that working excessive hours led 12.8% of them to lose enough sleep to result in underperformance at work(Åkerstedt 1). The lost rest would have definite negative impact on the fatigued workers, leading workers to become more inefficient (Sousa-Poza 1). At the same time, it is important to consider issues at this point. They potentially could lose sleep due to staying out with family and friends, as well as other leisurely activities. Even taking that into account, there is a statistically significant impact that long work hours have on one's sleep and health.

Another issue that arises with working more extended hours is that it places workers at a higher risk of injury on the job. The trucking industry exemplifies this due to the constant threat that is present while driving. An article was published in the Journal of Public Health Policy found that truck drivers work excessively long hours and that this was leading to more accidents on the road (Braver 341). Federal regulations in the United States say a truck driver can not work more than 10 hours a day, though working above that limit is a common practice motivated by reduced wages, with companies often overlooking it. Though it goes unstated, it can be inferred that some companies support it. This is likely because the drivers are significantly increasing their bottom line, more than enough to offset the extra wages that companies pay. This leads to some severe consequences, with the fatigue from long hours leading to significantly more vehicle crashes. Regrettably, both drivers and bystanders will be negatively affected by increasing amounts of motor vehicle accidents.

There is an argument to be made that extended work hours does not lead to any illnesses or diseases, such that the impact of long work hours on one's health should be ignored. For example, a study written by researchers in the UK found that there was no correlation between long work hours and an individual's risk of developing cancer (Heikkila 3). The fact remains that excessive work hours does not directly cause any illnesses or diseases for the worker. The fault in the argument lies in that it ignores the significance of the stress and job-specific risks that do in fact result from long work hours. Extensive amounts of work will not result in one developing debilitating diseases, but the stress that builds leads to serious health risks. It stands to reason that because of this, the argument can be refuted.

Finally, employers stand to lose as much as employees if their employee's health is not taken care of. They are put at a disadvantage due to two reasons: workers tend to be inefficient when they work longer, and heavy schedules invoke massive job turnover. The book Labor Economics points out that our entire work model is geared toward people working "inefficient long hours" because work hours is the method most employers use to measure productivity (Sousa-Poza 2). The fact that they use work hours to measure productivity leads people to work an extensive amount, though inefficiently, to impress their employers, but in doing so become fatigued and damage their health as a result of improper care (Marcia 3). In contrast, if people have to work significantly long hours due to labor schedules imposed by their employers, it pushes people to their physical limit and increases the number of turnovers for a job (Huselid 3). In a sense, this is beneficial for the well-being of the employee due to the worker being able to move on. Of course, this benefit is limited by their need to self-sustain themselves, showing that turnovers are situationally detrimental to the employee. In contrast, the employer loses out no matter the situation due to turnovers. Overall, working more extended hours has a negative impact on one's physical health to a great extent.

IMPACT OF LONG WORK HOURS ON HAPPINESS

In addition to physical well-being, excessively long work hours also have a profound impact on one's happiness. First of all, working long hours could diminish happiness due to taking time away from other aspects of one's life, such as friends and family. Secondly, working substantial amounts of hours to bolster capital could improve their quality of life. At the same time, one might work overtime not out of free will but out of necessity, due to exceptional circumstances. Financial need or personal pursuits could push one to work overtime even if they would not otherwise. Additionally, their job could potentially entail them needing to work overtime.

  A survey done on the British workforce found that working more extended hours leads to "negative job-to-home spillover" (White 1) among workers, which is an essential factor on the impact of working more extended hours on worker happiness. The spillover results from when people bring their work home with them to finish up or get ahead on the next day's work. This has significant implications since employers are getting free labor and employees are sacrificing their time. It lays out a back and forth relationship, where each is competing for the individual's time. The time the employee loses out on time that could have been spent doing something they find purpose and fulfillment in, such as spending time with friends and family.

  Another aspect to consider would be the impact of the extra capital one would gain from working overtime. In Alberta, over-time pay consists of one and a half times one's hourly wage ("Overtime Hours and Overtime Pay"). In Adam Smith's The Wealth of Nations, he makes a note of the fact that at "intervals of his leisure" (Smith 118), workers are reasonably likely to work a second job for the additional income. This leads to a situation where one could work for more extended hours and make significantly more money, where one could put the extra money towards something that would improve their overall quality of life. Potentially they would also use it for an external purpose, and not spend the money on themselves. Regardless the argument falls short based on the fact that people who work overtime tend to do it out of financial necessity and not out of free will (Golden 1).

The issue of working long hours due to external needs goes even further. The healthcare industry exemplifies this, where workers routinely work long hours due to patient needs and to no benefit of their own. An article written for JONA's Healthcare Law, Ethics, & Regulation discussed cases where nurses would work eight-hour shifts, but due to short staffing, end up working sixteen-hour shifts (Bosek 2). The potential issues that arise with extremely long changes play a massive detriment to the worker's happiness and well-being. At the same time, there is a bias in the healthcare industry to prioritize the wellbeing of patients over workers resulting in this outcome. Overall working long hours results in one needing to sacrifice their happiness.

SOLUTION AND LIMITATIONS

Moving forward, overall long working hours has a negative impact on one's well being. There is evidence that suggests it damages both a worker's physical health and happiness. A potential solution would to merely enforce laws that limit the amount that one could work, but this ignores the root of the issue. It is essential to consider the causes of why there is a trend towards working more extended hours. The initial answer that would be regarded as would likely be either crediting it to our current economic recession or the job market (Zagorsky). A better solution would tackle the heart of the problem, and it has to deal with why we work at all.

The foundations of job specialization are built on society's needs for the work to be done, such as a doctor protecting their patient's health. Additionally, the lack of the individual to support them self, and the potential for one to further their social standing, such as working excessive amounts to qualify for a promotion. The most long-lasting and comprehensive solutions would take into account the motivations behind working long hours in the first place.

    Another potential solution would be to build social safety-nets for the workforce so no one would ever need to work long hours. This could conceivably be done by introducing a universal basic income ("Basic income"). This would remove the need for workers to overwork themselves to meet their basic needs because all of them are provided. This, of course, has its limitations; it would not be feasible for a government it introduce it due to the red tape and backlash they would receive from taxpayers. It would be important to consider questions such as how it will be paid for and by who. At the same time, governments might have no issue with the backlash and would only hesitate due to the potential that working becomes unneeded. A better solution would introduce a less extreme safety net and take into consideration people who are required to work overtime, such as healthcare workers by subsidizing them and improving work conditions.

    A notable limitation of this argument as a whole is that zeroing in on the impacts of long work hours is that a lot of assumptions need to be taken. Reality is a lot messier, situations such active efforts from individuals to negate the negative impacts, such as by trying to eat better and sleeping more, would arise. Beyond the scope of this essay would be taking into consideration family and friend support systems that workers have, among other aspects such as differing lifestyles.

    In conclusion, the extent of the impact of working long hours on one's well-being is significantly negative. Tackling this issue is above any one individual and will require communities to work together, and solving this issue is integral to building the best possible future for everyone.

Works Cited

Åkerstedt, Torbjörn, et al. "Workload and work hours in relation to disturbed sleep and

> fatigue in a large representative sample". *ScienceDirect,* Journal of Psychosomatic Research. Jul 2002. vol. 53, no. 1, pp. 585–588. Journal article. Accessed 5 Apr 2017. <www.sciencedirect.com/science/article/pii/S0022 399902004476>.

Baldwin, John R., et al. "Productivity: What Is It? How Is It Measured? What Has Canada's

> Performance Been Over the Period 1961 to 2012?". *Statistics Canada,* Statistics Canada. Sep 2014. no. 38. Report. Accessed 28 Mar 2017. <www.statcan.gc.ca/pub/15-206-x/15-206-x2014038-eng.htm>.

"Basic income". *Wikipedia,* Wikipedia. Web. Accessed 10 Apr 2017.

> <en.wikipedia.org/wiki/Basic_income>.

Bosek, Marcia. "Mandatory Overtime: Professional Duty, Harms, and Justice". *JONA's*

> *Healthcare Law, Ethics, & Regulation,* Journal of Nursing Administration. Dec 2001. vol. 3, no. 4, pp, 99-102. Journal article. Accessed 7 Apr 2017. <journals.lww.com/jonalaw/Citation/2001/12000/

Mandatory_Overtime__Professional_Duty,_Harms,_and.2.aspx>.

Braver, Elisa R., et al. "Long Hours and Fatigue: A Survey of Tractor-Trailer Drivers." Journal of

Public Health Policy. 1992. vol. 13, no. 3, pp. 341–366. Journal article. Accessed 5 Apr 2017. <www.jstor.org/stable/3342733>.

Burke, Ronald J. "Working to Live or Living to Work: Should Individuals and Organizations

Care?" Journal of Business Ethics. 2009. vol. 84, pp. 167–172. Journal article. Accessed 6 Apr 2017. <www.jstor.org/stable/40294782>.

Dababneh, Awwad J., et al. "Impact of added rest breaks on the productivity and well being of

workers". *Altmetric,* Ergonomics. 10 Nov 2010. Journal article. Accessed 9 Apr 2017. <www.tandfonline.com/doi/citedby/10.1080/00140 130121538?scroll=top&needAccess=true>.

Dalton, Dan. "What percentage of our lives are spent working?". *Reference,* Reference*. Web.

Accessed 9 Apr 2017. <www.reference.com/math/percentage-lives-spent-working-599e3f7fb2c88fca#>.

Dembe, A. E., et al. "The Impact of Overtime and Long Work Hours on Occupational Injuries and Illnesses: New Evidence from the United States." *Occupational and Environmental Medicine.* 2005. vol. 62, no. 9, pp. 588–597. Journal article. Accessed 5 Apr 2017. <www.jstor.org/stable/27732586>.

Golden, Lonnie. "To your happiness? Extra hours of labor supply and worker well-being".

ScienceDirect, The Journal of Socio-Economics. Apr 2006. vol. 35, no. 2, pp. 382–397. Journal Article. Accessed 5 Apr 2017. <www.sciencedirect.com/science/article/pii/S1053535705001691>.

Heikkila, Katriina, et al. "Long working hours and cancer risk: a multi-cohort study". *nature,*

British Journal of Cancer. 18 Feb 2016. Journal article. Accessed 22 Mar 2017. <www.nature.com/bjc/journal/v114/n7/full/bjc201 69a.html>.

Huselid, Mark A. "The Impact Of Human Resource Management Practices On Turnover,

Productivity, And Corporate Financial Performance". *Academy of Management,* Academy of Management Journal. 1 June 1995. vol. 38 no. 3. Journal article. Accessed 28 Mar 2017. <amj.aom.org/content/38/3/635.short>.

Jarvis, Crystal. "Survey: 70% of employees work overtime, skip lunch". *Bizjournal,*

Birmingham Business Journal. 15 May 2009. Survey. Accessed 6 Apr 2017. <www.bizjournals.com/birmingham/stories/2009/05/11/daily39.html>.

Miller, Howard. *We Can Do it!*. *Wikipedia*, Westinghouse Company's War Production

> Coordinating Committee. 1942. Artwork. Accessed 3 Apr 2017. <https://en.wikipedia.org/wiki/Rosie_the_Riveter>.

Nandi, Alita. "Working Hours, Work Identity and Subjective Wellbeing". *Institute for Social and*

> *Economic Research,* University of Essex. Dec 2015. no. 21. Research paper. Accessed 5 Apr 2017. <www.iser.essex.ac.uk/research/publications/working-papers/iser/2015-21.pdf>.

Nanda, Ravinder, and James J. Browne. "Hours of Work, Job Satisfaction and Productivity."

> Public Productivity Review. 1977. vol. 2, no. 3, pp. 46–56. Journal article. Accessed 8 Apr 2017. <www.jstor.org/stable/3380223>.

Oswald, Andrew J., et al. "Happiness and Productivity". *Warwick,* Journal of

> Labour Economics. 7 Aug 2015. vol. 33, no. 4. Journal article. Accessed 5 Apr 2017.

<www2.warwick.ac.uk/fac/soc/economics/staff/ds
groi/papers/manuscriptandappendix.pdf>.

"Overtime Hours and Overtime Pay". *Alberta Labour,* Government of Alberta. 27 Sep 2011.

Web. Accessed 10 Apr 2017. <work.alberta.ca/employment-standards/overtime-hours-and-overtime-pay.html>.

Smith, Adam. *An Inquiry into the Nature and Causes of the Wealth of Nations.* 9 March 1776.

Gutenberg, 6 Feb 2013. Book. Accessed 7 Apr 2017. <www.gutenberg.org/files/3300/3300-h/3300-h.htm#link2HCH0010>.

Sousa-Poza, Alfonso. "Asymmetric information about workers' productivity as a cause for

inefficient long working hours". *ScienceDirect,* Labour Economics. Dec 2003. vol. 10, no. 6, pp. 727–747. Journal article. Accessed 5 Apr 2017. <www.sciencedirect.com/science/article/pii/S0927537103000162>.

"The impact of WWII on women's work". *Women and Work,* GreenNet. Web. Accessed 7 Apr

2017. <www.striking-women.org/module/women-and-work/world-war-ii-1939-1945>.

Thompson, Derek. "A World Without Work." *The Atlantic*, Atlantic Media Company. 17 Aug

2015. Web. Accessed 5 Apr 2017. <www.theatlantic.com/magazine/archive/2015/07/world-without-work/395294>.

Uehat, Tetsunojo. "Long Working Hours and Occupational Stress-related Cardiovascular

Attacks Among Middle-aged Workers in Japan". Center for Academic Publications Japan, 1991. vol.20, pp.147-153. Research paper. Accessed 28 Mar 2017. <www.jstage.jst.go.jp/article/jhe1972/20/2/20_2_147/_pdf>.

White, Michael. "'High-performance' Management Practices, Working Hours and Work–Life

Balance". *Wiley Online Library.* 18 June 2003. vol. 41, no. 2, pp. 175–195. Journal article. Accessed 28 Mar 2017. <onlinelibrary.wiley.com/doi/10.1111/1467-8543.00268/full>.

"Who Invented Weekends?". *Wonderopolis.* 2017. Web. Accessed 9 Apr 2017.

<wonderopolis.org/wonder/who-invented-weekends>.

"World Happiness Report 2017". *World Happiness Report,* United Nations. 2017. Report.

Accessed 7 Apr 2017. <worldhappiness.report/>.

Zagorsky, Jay. "Column: I'm predicting an economic recession in 2017. Are you ready?". *The*

    Conversation, PBS. 3 Jan 2017. Web. Accessed 10 Apr 2017. <www.pbs.org/newshour/making-sense/get-ready-economic-recession-coming-2017/>.

Chapter 3. Automation: The Right Path Forward?

As I read through "A World Without Work" by Derek Thompson and "Address to the Nation on Labor Day" by Richard Nixon, it became clear to me that the pervading theme was that of the importance of work and employment, and the effect technology could have on it. While automation is the main theme in "A World Without Work", mentions of it can be seen in Nixon's speech, wherein he says "we must make sure that technology does not dehumanize work, but makes it more creative and rewarding for the people who will operate the plants of the future"(2). Also, Nixon's belief that the "work ethic is ingrained in the American character"(1), ties into Thompson's belief that the "sanctity and preeminence of work lie at the heart of the [America's] politics, economics, and social interactions" (52).

Introduction

Often defined as "the execution by a machine agent of a function that was previously carried out by a human" (Strauch 206), automation has come under debate in recent times over the wide-ranging effects it may have on our ideas of work and society as a whole. A recent study from Oxford University estimates that "47% of jobs are under threat of being automated" within the next 50 years in the USA alone (Brown 39). Previously, automation was seen as a taker of mostly blue-collar occupations, but it's now assumed the next surge of automation will result in a loss of countless white-collar jobs as well. These include the most-common occupations in the United States such as retail salespersons, cashiers, food and beverage servers, and office clerks which altogether employ over 15.4 million people or nearly 10 percent of the labor force (Thompson 54). With the threat of such high unemployment looming, many have begun to question how society will manage. While some belief "the end of wage labor will allow for a golden age of well-being"(Thompson 55), others fear the loss of the "the value of achievement [and] the morality of self-reliance" that has come to define the American work ethic (Nixon 2). With the onset of widespread automation approaching fast, the extent to which automation should be implemented as a substitute for human labor must be considered. This paper argues that automation should be applied to a considerable extent, as the effectiveness of automation will likely lead to many positive consequences but at a significant cost to many stakeholders involved.

EFFECTIVENESS OF AUTOMATION

Modern automated systems are typically described as having four functions: "They acquire information, analyze information, select actions based on that analysis, and implement the action, as needed" (Strauch 206). The degree to which each function is carried out varies across systems and is affected by their degree of independence from the operators. Automation is particularly well suited to a class of systems called "sociotechnical systems," which are "integrated human and machine entities" that, when functioning together, can address a range of problems unable to be solved by either individually (Strauch 206).

Well-known examples of sociotechnical systems include air travel and marine operations, which are involved tasks that benefit significantly from the mixture of human labor and technology used to operate them. The accuracy and reliability of automation, the complexity of the processes involved and the substantial consequences of human operator errors also contribute to the effectiveness of automation in this field. Nevertheless, automation can still be considered quite useful on its own. This can be seen in everyday chores such as dishwashing and house cleaning, where technology such as the dishwasher and vacuum have replaced the previously laborious undertakings (Smith and Anderson 12).

    Automation has its limits, however. "Human" characteristics such as empathy, understanding, and intuitiveness are things that programmers find ill-suited to automation. These traits are found in the high-skill sectors discussed earlier, such as health and education. Considering that jobs such as doctors and teachers increased by "4.8 million between 2001 and 2009" (Bughin et al.), it's clear that automation isn't effective when it comes to jobs requiring significant human interaction. Otherwise, they would likely experience job-losses being seen in other sectors such as manufacturing. Furthermore, it's been noted that many low-skill occupations such as food preparation, cleaning, and security services (Tüzeman and Willis 4) have proved to be too difficult to automate. In fact, the employment share of low-skill occupations rose from "15 percent in 1983 to 18 percent in 2012" (Tüzeman and Willis 4). Automation has proven to be very useful with and without humans in all but a few applications, meaning its economic impacts will be significant.

ECONOMIC IMPACTS

Automation allows higher efficiency and productivity since automated machines do not require wages and work 24 hours a day. This is most obvious from an employer's perspective. When comparing the most valuable American company in 1964, AT&T, to a modern telecommunications giant, Google, the economic benefits of automation can be seen. Back then, AT&T was worth $267 billion and employed 758,611 people; today, Google is worth $370 billion but employs a mere 55,000 employees (Thompson 53). Automation and advanced technology have allowed Google to operate at a more significant scale alongside a much more substantial net worth with less than a tenth of AT&T's workforce. Productivity and efficiency of automation results in a few benefits to workers as well. One claim is that automation can create more work indirectly than it displaces directly. For example, acknowledge the growth of industries such as hairdressing and bartending in the UK, which has developed as a result of the increased earnings automation has provided to workers in the past (Stewart et al. 4). Automation can also create work directly, such as jobs in the technology and research field; in the last 35 years, "two of the top ten fastest growing occupations in the UK," information technology managers and programmers, have been in this sector (Stewart et al. 7). Conversely, consider data from the United States that state only 5% of the jobs created between 1993 and 2013 actually came from "high tech" sectors like computing, software, or telecommunications and that 9 out of 10 workers in the US today are in occupations that existed 100 years ago (Thompson 54), meaning automation may not be creating as many new jobs as some think. If the new numbers that say 14.9 million new jobs will be created by 2027, albeit with a net loss of 9.8 million US jobs (Gownder et al.) are taken into consideration, there's strong support for the claim that automation will likely result in a loss of employment - at least for Americans.

  This leads to the premise of the argument against automation, which views the destabilizing effects of industrialization on the economy as too severe. Many mourn the loss of manufacturing jobs in the US, which have decreased by almost 5 million since 2000 (Thompson 53). Others worry about job losses in the UK, such as the 57% drop in some typists and a 50% drop in company secretaries between 1992 and 2014 (Stewart et al. 4). However, many in support of automation argue that this isn't the big picture and that opponents overestimate the real effects on jobs. Note that while the number of typists and secretaries was dropping in the UK, there was a 168% increase in care workers and a 580% increase in teaching and educational support assistants in the same timeframe (Stewart et al. 4). Lastly, the declining middle class has become a significant concern for countless people; as jobs are continually lost to automation, "downward mobility, underemployment, and unemployment" are bound to affect these workers (Smith and Anderson 52) considerably. This may result in a 45% unemployment crisis which will dwarf the 25% unemployment rate that crippled the US economy in the 1930's ("Humans"). Middle-income households only shared "43% of US aggregate wealth in 2014", down substantially from 62% in 1970 ("Middle Class" 4); automation will likely exacerbate this problem and significantly impact other issues in society.

SOCIETAL IMPLICATIONS

If the economy were to suffer negatively from the implementation of automation, Great Depression-like scenarios might play out across the United States. Many say that the effects of industrialization will likely be worse than this due to its "versatility and growing capabilities" as not just a few economic sectors will be targeted, but likely whole swaths will be (Smith and Anderson 10). Those who believe automation will benefit society argue that many sectors of the economy will be spared, namely those that require human interaction. However, some believe even jobs too complex for today's computers will eventually be automated, including fields as thought-intensive as law, in which automation could make significant inroads by 2025 resulting in numerous lawyers being out of work (Smith and Anderson 47). After countless workers were replaced in Youngstown by automation in the 1980's, "Depression, spousal abuse, and suicide all became much more prevalent" (Thompson 51); if the displacement of a few thousand workers resulted in such an unfavourable social situation, one could only guess the societal implications when millions are displaced in the near future. Many argue that by doing work, "people acquire much of their self-regard and establish their place in a community" (McMullen 7). President Nixon argued that citizens become "a better person by the act of working," and that the work ethic was an integral part of the success of the United States (1). As automation displaces more and more jobs, workers will be left searching for a sense of purpose and fulfillment as their skills become obsolete.

      Numerous supporters of automation eagerly await its spread into society. They cite how much automation has benefited consumers in the past and will likely due so in the future. As wages rise, consumers have more substantial disposable incomes to spend on their wants. Automation, along with partly being the reason consumers are paid more, also dramatically increases productivity at ever cheaper costs, reducing the prices of thousands of goods and services. For instance, US CPI data show that the rate of a TV "has fallen by 98% since 1950" (Stewart et al. 7). Opponents of automation may contradict this by arguing these cheaper costs come at the expense of the workers, although proponents will likely argue that as automation reduces costs, increased consumer spending power will "create new demand and new jobs" (Stewart et al. 9). Some believe it's possible that automation will eliminate traditional jobs and make possible a "new artisanal economy" centered around self-expression (Thompson 56). Supporters believe this will restore work to a more meaningful and purposeful task, that "parts of our existence can and will be handed off to technology" to allow humans to accomplish tasks they want to achieve (Smith and Anderson 60). While some politicians, for example, may argue that work already provides meaning and fulfillment to workers, a 2014 report of worker satisfaction found that almost "70 percent of Americans do not feel engaged by their current job" (Thompson 55). There's no doubt that automation will continue to expand and that stakeholders involved need to develop solutions for whatever it may bring.

SOLUTIONS

Although it's hard to predict precisely what precedence automation will have in the coming decades, it's confident that automation of numerous industries will continue. So, the solutions will need to center on efficiently implementing automation without significantly reducing human labor or damaging society.

Workers whose skills may become obsolete with increased automation need to be provided the proper education to acquire new skills. Future work with automation needs operators with "sufficient expertise" to effectively handle nonroutine operating phases and "adequately diagnose and respond to unexpected system failures" (Strauch 222). Governments need to collaborate with stakeholders involved to decide the kind of "pre-employment and post-employment training" institutions would need to offer to allow these workers to keep pace with these technological developments as a result of automation (Wong). The educational system must prepare students for life with automation; the jobs most likely not to have been displaced will be those that require critical thought and comprehensive knowledge, so only the most well-educated humans will be ensured good employment. A more efficient education system may also help decrease the decline of the middle class, which would need to be redefined as its workforce is supplemented by automation.

Thompson believes governments should create more "ambitious community centers or other public spaces" where citizens can socialize while learning new skills or bonding around sports or crafts (59). Future work may need to center around places like these, where those who have lost their jobs to automation can pursue more meaningful lives and possibly contribute to society through their inventions or thoughts. Eventually, governments will need to find a solution to these large numbers of people displaced by automation. This is where the support for a "universal basic income" comes in. If a base income is provided to all citizens, people will be able to pursue work that they believe provides them fulfillment, and allows them to either work or live alongside automated systems. One way to provide this income is given by Thompson; he believes that government should "more heavily tax the growing share of income going to the owners of capital" and use that money to allocate a set income to citizens (60). An obvious limitation of this idea is what will happen if this portion of the population decides it is tired of supplying this revenue.

Automation is arguably one of the most significant issues of the coming decades and may end up defining the 21st century. Generally speaking, automation will need to be embraced to a reasonable extent, as some of its consequences will be harsh, but the overall promise it holds has the chance to revolutionize society for the better.

WORKS CITED

Brown, Kevin J. "What Is Your Narrative? Human Purpose and the Future of Work". *A World without Work? Technology, Automation, and the Future of Work.* Edited and with an introduction by Tyler Castle, 2016, pp. 37-49.
www.filepicker.io/api/file/oVtLEs5RSquQlguvJsKg. Accessed 27 March 2017.

Bughin, Jacques, et al. "A Future That Works: Automation, Employment, And Productivity". *McKinsey Global Institute,* January 2017.
www.forrester.com/report/The+Future+Of+Jobs+2025+Working+Side+By+Side+With+Robots/-/E-RES119861. Accessed 28 March

"Humans Need Not Apply". *Youtube,* uploaded by CGP Grey, 13 August 2014.
www.youtube.com/watch?v=7Pq-S557XQU&feature=youtu.be

Gownder, J. P., et al. "The Future Of Jobs, 2027: Working Side By Side With Robots". *Forrester Research,* 3 April 2017.
www.forrester.com/report/The+Future+Of+Jobs+2025+Working+Side+By+Side+With+Robots/-/E-RES119861. Accessed 29 March 2017.

McMullen, Steven. "The Impossibility and Challenge of a World without Work". *A World without Work? Technology, Automation, and the Future of Work.* Edited and with an introduction by Tyler Castle, 2016, pp. 3-12.

www.filepicker.io/api/file/oVtLEs5RSquQlguvJsKg. Accessed 27 March 2017.

Nixon, Richard. "Address to the Nation on Labor Day.", Online by Gerhard Peters and John T. Woolley, The American Presidency Project , 6 September 1971, Camp David, Maryland. http://www.presidency.ucsb.edu/ws/?pid=3138. Accessed 19 March 2017.

Smith, Aaron, and Janna Anderson. "AI, Robotics, and the Future of Jobs. *Pew Research Centre*, 6 August 2014. www.pewinternet.org/2014/08/06/future-of-jobs/. Accessed 27 March 2017.

Stewart, Ian, et al. "Technology and people: The great job-creating machine". *Deloitte LLP*, 2015. www2.deloitte.com/content/dam/Deloitte/uk/Documents/finance/deloitte-uk-technology-and-people.pdf. Accessed 28 March 2017.

Strauch, Barry. "The Automation-by-Expertise-by-Training Interaction: Why Automation-Related Accidents Continue to Occur in Sociotechnical Systems". *Measuring Safety and Performance in Human–Automation Systems: Theories, Metrics, and Practice,* vol. 59, no. 2, 2017, pp. 204-228. *SAGE journals,* doi:10.1177/0018720816665459. Accessed 28 March 2017.

The American Middle Class is Losing Ground: No longer the majority and falling behind financially.".

Pew Research Centre, Washington D.C., 9 December 2015. www.pewsocialtrends.org/2015/12/09/the-american-middle-class-is-losing-ground/. Accessed 30 March 2017.

Thompson, Derek. "A World Without Work". *The Atlantic*, July/August 2015. www.theatlantic.com/magazine/archive/2015/07/world-without-work/395294/. Accessed 19 March 2017.

Tüzeman, Didem and Jonathan Willis. "The Vanishing Middle: Job Polarization and Workers' Response to the Decline in Middle-Skill Jobs". *Journalist's Resource*, May 2013. journalistsresource.org/wp-content/uploads/2013/05/Tuzemen-Willis.pdf. Accessed 28 March 2017.

Chapter 4. To What Extent Should Secondary Education Be Pursued?

Introduction

In the early 1900s, the purpose of a college education was to gain a Licence of Instruction, to teach at public schools, but even back then, average families were not able to afford the cost. (Thelin) However, times changed and college became a necessary part of life or often regarded utmost importance. With nearly 20.5 million students attending American colleges and universities, universities are currently seen as a vital step in life rather than an optional one. (NCES) Thus when an average American annual increase of $280 for university tuition is introduced many secondary education students often find themselves falling into crippling debt. (Trends In Higher Education) The question of whether or not a college education is worth the money is a relevant issue that plagues many of us, individually high school students. Opening new opportunities, allows a person to grow, however, is it worth the cost of debt and the chance of unemployment and underemployment? (Nixon)

Debt and Money

Americans bear $1.3 trillion in student debt; more and more Wall Street and private equity companies peddle loans and collected fees from the government. (Steele, Williams) These types of loans often lead to private companies gaining more money instead of students paying off loans. Additionally missing or being late for loan payments adds additional fees and lowers credit score. Thus students often find themselves in crippling debt and struggle to make necessary purchases or gain employment. (Mitchell) However, college graduates make more money, the median income for families with a bachelor's degree holder was $100,096 in 2011. (Baum, Ma, Pays) Degree holders are able, over a period of time to pay back their student debt and make more money than the average high school degree holder. In fact, 85% of the Forbes 2012 America's most precious 400 were college graduates, proving that not only were college students able to pay back student loans but also rise to one of the wealthiest in a wealthy nation. (Fontevecchia) Others may believe loan repayment to be ineffective, those borrowers who began compensation after graduation, only 40 percent were able to make the agreed payments while 25 percent became delinquent and 15 percent defaulted. ("NACBA") The remaining 20% participated in programs that allowed them to postpone or reduce payments. Though this may be the case, more and more jobs are requiring college degrees, it is estimated that by 2020, 65% of all industrial jobs will need postsecondary education. (Recovery: Job Growth and Education 3)

    This puts college graduates at an advantage in the job market as they are able qualify for more higher paying jobs. Furthermore, though the debt is often much, only 1% of those with a bachelor's degree rely on the Food Stamp Program compared to 8% of high school graduates, similar statistics can be found for the National School Lunch Program. (Baum, Ma, Pays) Since such a small number rely on national food programs, the majority of college graduates can feed themselves and survive until a job opportunity arises. Presumably, for young college graduates, the unemployment rates stand at 8.8% and underemployment is at 18.3%. (Finio, Sabadish, Shierholz) These rates are considerably low, meaning that the majority of university graduates are employed and making income, though this type of work may be hard, degree holders are still better off than those without a degree.

A study found that the more the participants' income level increases, the more their self-esteem increases. (Ummet) Because college graduates make more than the average high school graduate, they should feel more comfortable, valuable and active. (Ummet) Therefore the need for real wage increases leads to a better life. (Nixon)

HEALTH INSURANCE AND PENSION PLANS

As stated by Nixon, the need for medical care and a secure retirement are "taking their place alongside the needs we are more familiar with." (Nixon) Among full-time, year-round workers ages 25 and older, 70% of four-year college graduates were offered pension plans by their employers in 2008; while only 55% of high school graduates were offered plans. (Baum, Ma, Payea) Pension plans are necessary to increase retirement confidence or "secure retirement" (Nixon) and lower costs placed on the government which ultimately leads to more taxpayers dollars being spent. (Sebastiano) College degree holders have a substantially higher probability of receiving pension plans. The gap between high school graduates and college graduates is increasingly noticeable as 68% of four-year college graduates working in the private sector were covered by employer-provided health insurance. (Baum, Ma, Payea) Only 50% of high school graduates were covered by employer health insurance. (Baum, Ma Payea) Being able to secure health insurance or a pension is vital to the needs of an American worker and by going to college, the chances of receiving a plan increases.

However, the difference is also affected by drops in employer coverage. Pension coverage in high school students dropped from 9.7 percent to 5.9 percent. (Finio, Sabadish, Shierholz) Over the same period, employed young college graduates who receive pension coverage from their employer dropped from 41.5 percent to 27.2 percent. (Finio, Sabadish, Shierholz) Though the drop between the years for college graduates has increased, bachelor degree holders still hold a higher percentage of having pension plans than those of high school degrees.

Opponents may say, that most employers believe most college graduates have the skills and knowledge for entry-level positions, but less than half think they have what is required for advancement and promotion to higher levels. (Hart Research) Arguably, this means that college graduates are often working first jobs with the chance of promotion, higher pay and more benefits being less than half. On the other hand, graduates who work first jobs gain experience and confidence in their work along with networking value. 65% to 80% of jobs are found through networking, giving college students participate in internships, campus events and access to alumni networks. (Harvard Business) In any case, university graduates accumulate networking value and experience in their respective fields which eventually leads to job satisfaction and higher pay.

VALUE OF DEGREES

In 1973, 28% of jobs were held by postsecondary graduates and by 2020, 65% of all industrial jobs will require postsecondary education. (Recovery: Job Growth and Education 3) The United States of America is becoming more educated, and a university is growing more crucial to finding employment. With more students applying for university, the percentage of bachelor degrees rose to 33.4 percent in 2016, a "significant milestone since ... 1940," said Kurt Bauman, Chief of the Education. (Highest Educational Levels Reached) Within the significant increase of amounts of Bachelor's, Master's and Ph.D. degrees, it presents a new issue; the value of college degrees has decreased. Moreover, the competition for positions in the labor force has grown harsh, with nearly 5 million increase in people with Master's degrees. (Coleman) Though the game is fierce, a college degree still a statement to the employer and often what employers look for to thin out the competition, deeming university necessary to meet the pre-requirements. (Coleman)

Even within the community, a 1% increase in college graduates spikes the wages of those without a high school diploma by 1.9%. (Baum, Ma, Pays) This implies that the value of a college degree is respected enough to cause a wage increase in those without a degree. College graduates end up attracting higher paying employers to those communities and create mutualistic benefits to the employers and degree holders. Additionally, graduates who were previously participated in a funded internship program and received a full job offer had a higher starting wage than high school graduates or unpaid internship. (Student Survey Report 41) This may be because of the job training required to improve skills, and productivity, by increasing productivity more objectives can be accomplished. (Nixon) In conclusion, though a young worker is starting out their career may not always get the highest pay, through the value of a college degree are they able to gain what they want. (Nixon)

CONCLUSION

Gaining a college degree is time-consuming and stressful, but the risks of it do eventually pay off. A possible option is to lower the cost of universities or remove for-profit colleges. Some of those universities see degree programs as easy money and can monetize their brand as a university by offering "professional" 1-year programs. (Carey) These programs are often expensive with lax admission requirements allowing students to enter the job market with false academic credentials. (Carey) If the price of public and or private universities is lowered, more students with the requirements can enter and thus decrease the worth of profiting universities and increase the number of students with proper credentials. However, this brings up the issue of the value of bachelor's degree being diluted. If universities were to raising the admission criteria and lower the number of students allowed in, then their quality of students would increase.

Additionally, employers would be more likely to seek these students as they will usually have a more extensive skill set to meet the higher admission averages. But this would create a more significant gap between the post-secondary educated and those who have a high school degree, spurring more students to enter university for a better job or higher wage. Artisans and other types of creative skill-based jobs would face a massive drop severely changing the culture of western life. At any rate, the best option would be to enter university to pursue a degree for a job that one is passionate about. This way students will have the motivation to complete degrees and find a suitable job. Perhaps if the pay of skilled labor is raised, universities will be able to accept more students that have dreams that require degrees and other high school graduates in specific trades will be able to catch up with university students.

WORKS CITED

Brown, Kevin J. "What Is Your Narrative? Human Purpose and the Future of Work". *A World without Work? Technology, Automation, and the Future of Work.* Edited and with an introduction by Tyler Castle, 2016, pp. 37-49. www.filepicker.io/api/file/oVtLEs5RSquQlguvJsKg. Accessed 27 March 2017.

Bughin, Jacques, et al. "A Future That Works: Automation, Employment, And Productivity". *McKinsey Global Institute,* January 2017. www.forrester.com/report/The+Future+Of+Jobs+2

025+Working+Side+By+Side+With+Robots/-/E-RES119861. Accessed 28 March

"Humans Need Not Apply". *Youtube*, uploaded by CGP Grey, 13 August 2014. www.youtube.com/watch?v=7Pq-S557XQU&feature=youtu.be

Gownder, J. P., et al. "The Future Of Jobs, 2027: Working Side By Side With Robots". *Forrester Research*, 3 April 2017. www.forrester.com/report/The+Future+Of+Jobs+2025+Working+Side+By+Side+With+Robots/-/E-RES119861. Accessed 29 March 2017.

McMullen, Steven. "The Impossibility and Challenge of a World without Work". *A World without Work? Technology, Automation, and the Future of Work.* Edited and with an introduction by Tyler Castle, 2016, pp. 3-12. www.filepicker.io/api/file/oVtLEs5RSquQlguvJsKg. Accessed 27 March 2017.

Nixon, Richard. "Address to the Nation on Labor Day.", Online by Gerhard Peters and John T. Woolley, The American Presidency Project , 6 September 1971, Camp David, Maryland. http://www.presidency.ucsb.edu/ws/?pid=3138. Accessed 19 March 2017.

Smith, Aaron, and Janna Anderson. "AI, Robotics, and the Future of Jobs. *Pew Research Centre*, 6 August 2014.

www.pewinternet.org/2014/08/06/future-of-jobs/. Accessed 27 March 2017.

Stewart, Ian, et al. "Technology and people: The great job-creating machine". *Deloitte LLP*, 2015. www2.deloitte.com/content/dam/Deloitte/uk/Documents/finance/deloitte-uk-technology-and-people.pdf. Accessed 28 March 2017.

Strauch, Barry. "The Automation-by-Expertise-by-Training Interaction: Why Automation-Related Accidents Continue to Occur in Sociotechnical Systems". *Measuring Safety and Performance in Human–Automation Systems: Theories, Metrics, and Practice,* vol. 59, no. 2, 2017, pp. 204-228. *SAGE journals,* doi:10.1177/0018720816665459. Accessed 28 March 2017.

The American Middle Class is Losing Ground: No longer the majority and falling behind financially.". *Pew Research Centre,* Washington D.C., 9 December 2015. www.pewsocialtrends.org/2015/12/09/the-american-middle-class-is-losing-ground/. Accessed 30 March 2017.

Thompson, Derek. "A World Without Work". *The Atlantic*, July/August 2015. www.theatlantic.com/magazine/archive/2015/07/world-without-work/395294/. Accessed 19 March 2017.

Tüzeman, Didem and Jonathan Willis. "The Vanishing Middle: Job Polarization and Workers' Response to the Decline in Middle-Skill Jobs". *Journalist's Resource*, May 2013. journalistsresource.org/wp-content/uploads/2013/05/Tuzemen-Willis.pdf. Accessed 28 March 2017.

Chapter 5. Using Creativity to Understand Western Political Health in the Past Half a Millenia: Do Paint Strokes Mirror Pen Strokes?

Introduction

Politics within the last half a millennia has changed in numerous ways, as significant shifts in the Western political structure have been prevalent in events such as the French Revolution; its ideals of liberty and equality can be seen through the art of the era embodying enlightenment ideals("Neo-classicism and the French Revolution"). Thus it is quite likely that such reflections occurring in the themes of creative thinking could be an indicator towards the overall political health of a region. In this case, political health would encompass ideas such as legitimacy, stability, and trust in the government. The importance of gaining further understanding of history's politics comes in the form of Historical context, as it plays a large role in modern-day social research by bringing explanation for certain phenomena and widens research by "suggesting new ways of studying old questions"(Lawrence).

In this case, creative thought can indicate the state of a system in two ways with its themes. Either by thematically commenting on the government or by showing the artist's ideas and subsequently the environment in which they are in. This connection between creative thought as art and the political health of a region is what raises the question of how can an original idea be looked at best to understand the political health of a part in the western world to know how this could deal with modern day issues.

THE GOVERNMENT IN ART

Art has been able to display the truthfulness of the legitimacy of a regime. In The Last Judgement by Michelangelo, it is pointed out by Bernadine Barnes, a professor of Renaissance Art History at Wake Forest University, that nearly all of the ideas came from the artist himself. As Pope Clement VII and Paull III were the facilitators of the piece, they "allowed the idea to be brought to completion" (Barnes 54), suggesting that while the ideas were effectively filtered, they still were coming from Michelangelo himself. Additionally, the painting was created in a time of "ideological rigidity"(Hammer), as the Church's power was waning under the influence of money. Therefore, in how the painting displays higher members of the clergy in comfortable clothing, it becomes "traditional and extremely innovative"(Barnes 44). Also, it is known that the criticism given for the painting during the period of its unveiling was incredibly narrow and only focused on superficial aspects such as the nudity, and it's broader implications have remained unexplored until recently (Hammer). This innovation may also be due to Michelangelo likely being a devout Catholic as he previously worked on the Sistine Chapel. However, the lack of criticism is still unexplained. Thus, it can be inferred, with context indicated by the rich clothing of the clergy depicted, that the Church as an institution was forcing people to believe in their legitimacy at the time.

    In addition to showing the reality of the legitimacy of a regime, art can display the inadequacy of a regime's ability to provide for their people as well. In Courbet's The Stone Breakers, he presents a realistic image of two people working in a harsh environment in poor and ripped clothing. The piece famously gives the young and the old in such a situation to suggest that "working-class life is an endless cycle"(Graev), noted by a piece published in Discoveries from Cornell's Knight Institute for Writing in the Disciplines. The painting is a commentary on the harshness that the working-class during Courbet's time had to work through during the Industrial Revolution. During this period while the economy flourished, the living conditions of the people were poor as in neighboring Britain, life expectancy fell to 25 years. Also the height of people, which can indicate multiple factors of quality of life, amongst the English soldiers hit a low during this period, and only grew back during the latter half of the 19th century when advance was made in public health and food safety. This kind of effect can be seen too in France as the effects of the Industrial Revolution reached all throughout Europe ("Did living standards improve during the Industrial Revolution?.") and the height growth amongst the French dipped and grew similarly to the English (Komlos). Using the data combined with the message of the painting; the artist is communicating that workers are trapped and have no way of leaving the workforce, but the work is profoundly impacting their health. This exposes how incompetent the government was at dealing with such issues and indicates an inadequate consideration of people's rights during the time of the Industrial Revolution.

However, artists' perspectives can be quite biased towards one side, as shown in Russia right around the revolution there was an entire generation of artists that fervently supported revolutionary ideas. Noted by Martin Sixsmith, a former BBC correspondent for Russia during its Soviet days, the art during the revolution carried promises "of brave new worlds and liberation from the past" (Sixsmith). Artists of the time were in love with the revolution and went so far as to produce street art "celebrating the revolution and denouncing its foes"(Sixsmith). This form of action displays the political bias of the artists during this time, and such bias can be seen elsewhere as well with the inclusion of enlightenment thought in the neo-classicism arts that dominated France during the French Revolution ("Neo-classicism and the French Revolution."). However in both these cases, they were during times of extreme change, and both were during times when trust in the government is at a low, indicating to a lack of legitimacy. Therefore substantial scale bias only becomes significant in times of enormous change or political unrest, making it still indicative of political issues.

In all, art has a secure connection with government directly, as art as an expression is quite capable of providing commentary and displaying aspects of the governing body. Significant bias in the art would only show through during times of extreme change, therefore making bias useful for indication rather than not.

The Artist's Mind

Artists own opinions occasionally show in their art and provide their commentary on political situations, and those thoughts could help understand the stability of the case. According to John Suchet, a presenter of classical FM and a recipient of an honorary fellowship from the Royal Academy of Music for his work on Beethoven ("John's Honours."), Beethoven's Eroica Symphony was at one point dedicated for Napoleon. Upon hearing the news that Napoleon crowned himself emperor, he tore the title page in rage as he believed Napoleon would "trample on all the rights of man, and just satisfy his ambition" (Suchet). Beethoven then changed the title to "Heroic Symphony, composed to celebrate the memory of a great man"(Bratby). Not much later Europe was engulfed in a war against Napoleon(Driault). The prevalence of Beethoven's feelings taking control here was not much unlike the situation that was brewing in Europe of tense alliances forming to stop Napoleon from attempting to gain more power in Europe (Driault). Although Beethoven did at once agree with Napoleon's revolutionary ideals unlike many of the leaders of the time, it is clear that the war was started for Napoleon's want for power and that Beethoven's reaction reflected his desire for power with the name change. Thus, still being able to show that his beliefs were in a way indicative of the political stability of the region at the time.

    Not only can an artist's opinion indicate political stability, but it can also bring to light the perspective of entire groups about the ruling state. In Albert Camus's famous essay regarding the Myth of Sisyphus, he explores the idea of life without reason through Sisyphus himself. He argues that "one must imagine Sisyphus happy" (Camus) because "his fate belongs to him"(Camus). The essay was written and published while much of France was under the control of Nazi Germany, and Camus was a member of the resistance at the time ("Albert Camus - Biographical."). The theme of controlling fate is the reason for Sisyphus's absurd happiness, together with the situation of the times can be inferred to be a common idea amongst the resistance members. This inference is further supported by the popularity of the absurdist theatre between 1950 and 1970 and was primarily based on the absurdist ideas proposed by Albert Camus(Anderson). Through his art, Camus was able to reflect the beliefs of the resistance movement and subsequently the distrust they held for their puppet state.

However, aestheticism introduces the idea of "art for art's sake" (Pater 213). In Pater's conclusion to Studies in the History of the Renaissance, he argues for the idea that art driven by "the love of art for art's sake" (Pater 213) creates the highest quality of art. This idea is supported by the belief that experiences are "a swarm of impressions" (Pater 209), where passions derived from experience are only most strongly felt "for that moment only"(Pater 210). The use of sacrificing the art's quality for some "abstract morality we have not identified with ourselves, or what is only conventional, has no real claim upon us"(Pater 212). An example of such would be the works by Maurice Ravel. His Bolero is considered one of his most important pieces, yet it is a piece that was created from a passion for "art for art's sake"(Pater 213) where Ravel came upon a melody one day and decided to create a piece from it("The Story Of Ravel's Boléro."). Despite other pieces of work being much more politically interesting such as Miroirs(Murdoch),

Bolero remains as the piece that captures people the most now and back then. Thus showing that sometimes the most impactful pieces are not the most controversial, but rather the ones that inspire beauty the most. This is not the case for all pieces of work, or even as a major philosophy under most artists as even defenders of aestheticism do not believe it is usable in practice.

Defenders of the movement have claimed that only pursuing "aesthetic gratification" is absurd(Askari). As explored in the novel The Picture of Dorian Gray by Oscar Wilde, the pursuit of pure aestheticism would ultimately result in a "lack of remorse, self-absorption, and intellectual regression"(Duggan). Wilde's novel shows that pure aestheticism is incompatible with morality, and would require compromises to both sides to align the two together. Thus while aestheticism is a concept that is alive, it is not well, and most pieces of work do not follow a significant amount of its principles.

Altogether the implications of artist's thoughts appearing in their art can either be a direct commentary or a manifestation of the people's opinions. The case of aestheticism for the autonomy of art is not significant, as art for art's sake is considered absurd and impossible in specific art forms; lessening the impact on the usability of artist's beliefs to indicate political health.

SOLUTION

By looking at multiple examples throughout the last 500 years, it could be naively understood that art's themes can be used merely as a mirror to understand the political situation. This understanding could be sufficient in many cases. However, the existence of aestheticist principles and the knowledge that art is primarily for beauty make it unfit for every scenario. Thus the use of the technique as a sole indicator for political health is not recommended. However, it would be able to provide additional information in specific contexts to gain new and perhaps unknown perspectives on historical issues. To best use it for indicating political health an analyst must understand, to an extent, the artist and the period. The additional context would be able to allow for a fuller understanding of to what degree is the art for beauty's sake and to what degree it can be connected to the potential political issue.

    Using the ideas presented here to understand a current situation with automation can demonstrate the usefulness of the results. With automation significantly affecting the economy in practically removing the labor force, Derek Thompson from The Atlantic suggests that "the next wave of automation could return us to an age of craftsmanship and artistry."(Thompson). He argues that new manufacturing based on tech such as 3-D printing could create an "economy geared around self-expression"(Thompson). Indeed in areas such as makerspaces that promote "open-ended"(Forest et al.) styled projects for personal use. Such projects are geared around creation, and overarching themes would be for usability and function as "Personal-Engineering"(Forest et al.) types of projects are the most common types of non-class work done at a University Makerspace in Georgia Institute of Technology. The move away from traditional labor types of jobs and focus on creativity in the economy would require government intervention to smooth it better out to accommodate the people. Depending on the reaction to support makerspaces type institutions and their response to increasing unemployment, the growing self-supported creative DIY community being created may indicate towards a lack of rights given to the people.

WORKS CITED

"Albert Camus - Biographical." *Nobelprize.org*, 11 April 2017,

> www.nobelprize.org/nobel_prizes/literature/laureates/1957/camus-bio.html. Accessed 6 April 2017.

Anderson, Andrew. *The Violence of Identity Construction in French and Francophone Absurdist Theater.* Dissertation, Ohio State University, 2011.

Askari, Muhammad. "Art for Art's Sake." *The Annual of Urdu Studies,* vol. 27, 2012, Accessed

> 9 April 2017.

Barnes, Bernadine. *Michelangelo's Last Judgement: The Renaissance Response.* University

> of California Press, 1988, Accessed 5 April 2017.

Bratby, Richard. "Royal Liverpool Philharmonic Orchestra Programme Notes Online." *Liverpool Philharmonic,* www.prismic-io.s3.amazonaws.com/liverpoolphilharmonic%2F01ceed85-05a8-4460-9ad8-96aa966700c0_eroica+programme+notes.pdf. Accessed 8 April 2017.

Camus, Albert. "The Myth of Sisyphus." Justin O'Brien, *Hamish Hamilton,* 1995, Accessed 15

> March 2017.

"Did living standards improve during the Industrial Revolution?." *The Economist*, Sept. 13 2013,

    Accessed 8 April 2017.

    Driault, Edouard. "The Coalition of Europe Against Napolean." *The American Historical Review*, vol. 24, no. 4, 1996, www.jstor.org/stable/pdf/1835810.pdf. Accessed 8 April 2017.

    Duggan, Patrick. "The Conflict Between Aestheticism and Morality in Oscar Wilde's The Picture of Dorian Gray." *Boston University*,

    www.bu.edu/writingprogram/journal/past-issues/issue-1/duggan/. Accessed 8 April 2017.

Forest, Craig, et al. "The Invention Studio: A University Maker Space and Culture." *Advances in*

    Engineering Education, 2014, Accessed 4 April 2017.

Graev, Nicole. "The Body as a Sign of Class in Courbet's The Stone Breakers and Manet's

    Olympia." *Discoveries,* vol. 1, no. 2, 1995, Accessed 29 March 2017.

Hammer, Sam. "Reading Sixteenth-Century Italy through Michelangelo's Last Judgement."

    Discoveries, vol. 2, no. 6, 1997, Accessed 30 March 2017.

"John's Honours." *johnsuchet.co.uk*, 2014, Accessed 6 April 2017.

Komlos, John & Cinnirella, Francesca. "European in the Early 18th Century." *Volkswirtschaftliche Fakultat,* vol. 2005, no. 5, 2005, www.epub.ub.uni-muenchen.de/572/1/european_heights_in_the_early_18th_century.pdf. Accessed 8 April 2017.

Lawrence, Barbara. "Historical Perspective: Using the Past to Study the Present." *The Academy of Management Review*, vol. 9, no.2, April 1984, pp. 307-312, Accessed 4 April 2017.

Murdoch, Heloise. *Ravel's Mirrors: Text and Context.* Dissertation, University of the Witwatersrand, 2007.

"Neo-classicism and the French Revolution." *Oxford Art Online*, 25 Sept. 2016, www.oxfordartonline.com/public/page/themes/neoclassicismandthefrenchrevolution. Accessed 6 April 2017.

Pater, Walter. *The Renaissance Studies in Art and Poetry.* MacMilland and Co, 1888.

Sixsmith, Martin. "The story of art in the Russian Revolution.", *Royal Academy of Arts,* 20 Dec. 2016, Accessed 7 April 2017.

Suchet, John. *Beethoven: The Man Revealed.* Atlantic Monthly Press, 2012.

"The Story Of Ravel's Boléro." *ClassicFM,* Accessed 6 April 2017.

Thompson, Derek. "A World Without Work." *The Atlantic,* July 2015, Accessed 8 April 2017.

Chapter 6. What are the Effects of Automation on Cultural Works?

Throughout most of history, self-expression has been limited to material things. The advent of the printing press was a revolution. It changed a world where scribes had to scribble away for months to replicate works to one wherein a whole job could be done in a day. This allowed authors to spread their actions to others beyond just a handful. Still, there was a limit to copies produced and distribution of those copies throughout Europe, and the works were vulnerable to the passage of time. Later, the future revolutions of movies, radio and television were limited in another way. They were facilitated by organizations that only had so much regarding frequencies and airtime to distribute works and as such most often did not promote amateur jobs. Recently the technology of the internet has changed that. Any aspiring artist can upload their work to be viewed by all, and any writer can place their words publicly online to be read by any person. But even now a more significant change than the internet is conceivable. As machines grow more capable of performing routine work the future of humans within this kind of work is becoming ever more in question as technology replaces the jobs of numerous workers it appears that human society is about to have more free time than ever before. Indeed the capstone source A World Without Work cites an Oxford study that projects machines will be able to perform half of all jobs in America in the next two decades (Thompson). While this figure is impressive, it doesn't bring any context to how many of these jobs will be lost because of the advent of automation. Still, it makes clear how human civilization is going to change over the course of this century. Amusingly enough Derek Thompson argues that the study he cited didn't go far enough. Noting that research has been done suggesting that phycology patients may be more willing to talk about their problems to a computer implying that some intellectual jobs are already replaceable. This shows just "how easily computers can encroach on areas previously considered "for humans only" (Thompson). This versatility makes it hard to predict how far-reaching the impact of a machine workforce will be. It is conceivable that over the course of the next few centuries the vast bulk of jobs will be automated leaving people with spare time to do as they choose. Of course "most jobs that exist today will exist in some form." as only the "elevator operator" has been utterly replaced (Younge). After all, someone still needs to program the coffee machine to make a proper beverage. Such an opinion may hold valid for as long as corporations prefer human labor to devices. Even so, regular jobs will likely be reduced to a few custodians of the machines and the occasional artisan. Still, the question begs what people will choose to do with their time?

Spare Time

It is worth remarking the amount of time that is spent on work by the average person. A recent study published by Gallup found that forty-seven hours a week or around twenty-eight percent of a person's week is spent on a job(Saad). A natural side effect of this time becoming spare time is that people will be more capable of mastering their respective hobbies to a higher degree. On average, according to a survey from the U.S. Census Bureau, the average time spent in recreational activities is around five to six hours per day working for approximately thirty-eight hours (Statista). With the later average being roughly eighty percent of the former you could argue that recreation time for the average citizen will be doubled. How that plays into increases in time spent on hobbies is questionable as there is another time sink for the average American...the Fool's Lantern.

AN ASSAULT ON REPETITION

Around thirty-eight hours and twenty-three minutes, a week are spent looking at screens by the average American in 2013 (Nielsen). It is possible that among these hours of works the creations that remain constant in interactions, whether between the audience and the story or are merely within the story will lose staying power. Such works as large reality tv series with a constant premise will fade away because of the human trait of novelty. The desire of innovation is deeply ingrained within the human species affecting individuals as young as a year old. More relevantly is a study surveying nine hundred and eighteen individuals broken into four survey groups about what was important to them on their vacations. Among these questions "I like to find myself at destinations where I can explore new things" was asked to which 73% of the sample size responded affirmatively (Tae-Hee). It is worth noting other questions belonging to the same category of "Change from Routine" such as "My ideal vacation involves looking at things I have not seen before" and "I feel a powerful urge to explore the unknown on vacation" scored substantially lower. The problems that these questions face in understanding the extent of novelty in humans is in word choices such as "ideal" and "sense." 'Ideal vacation' brings in a myriad of other factors such as relatives and revisiting places with old memories. Given how pressed for time vacations often are especially given that this paper deals with Americans who under the Fair Labour Standards Act have no paid vacation time (DOL) and thus the idea of the finite vacation is pressing on the surveyed. The ideal vacation cannot be indefinite. This makes it so the question must score lower. "I feel a powerful urge to explore the unknown on vacation" is even worse as it describes a strong emotion that doesn't come close to resembling the milder psychological pressure of "Like to . . . Explore" that people feel and thus is naturally less well received. Moving back to the primary topic as novelty appears to affects people on vacation any change in behavior in a post-work world must be explained in a difference in behavior between vacation and the grind of work as such social contexts will be treated differently by the people living in them. The Capstone source The Myth of Sisyphus argues "the workman of today works every day in his life at the same tasks, and this fate is no less absurd. But it is tragic only at the rare moments when it becomes conscious" (Camus). To Albert Camus, the worker is unconscious; unaware of how absurd their fate is to eke out a living mindlessly performing the same tasks for the duration of their working lives. This inert nature of the working class one acclimatized to drudgery would explain why after work the desire to pursue novel ideas would be dulled. Force of habit maintains a mindset where the pursuit of innovative concepts isn't on the minds of the workforce. Therefore remove the social norms of tedious work and what should be left is a world where the simplistic and repetitive finds itself lacking an audience.

EMOTION AND THE SPREAD OF IDEAS

Supreme court justice Oliver Wendell Holmes once claimed that "the best test of truth is the power of [a] thought to get itself accepted in the competition of the market (Homes)." This invisible hand of ideas gels well with a capitalist worldview where people ultimately act in a manner that favors the welfare of others. But the elegant marketplace of ideas breaks down before human nature. A Princeton experiment testing for shareability of stories found that while "the ratings of whether a story occurred and could occur were highly correlated." After controlling for some perceptions of stories that influenced shareability stories rated to invoke interest they were 49% more likely to be rated as something the reader would share. This shows just how much of an effect emotions have on what gets passed on. This means that what people feel about work can affect how they portray that work to others. An excellent example of this would be the capstone source. We Can Do It. (Miller) Its original purpose was just another poster in a series trying to keep people working for the war effort, but it became so much more. Rediscovered it became an icon of feminist ideals and found new meaning and purpose to the point where a description for a "Rosie the Riveter" stamp emphasizes it as belonging to a progressive history that the artist probably never anticipated would exist (U.S. Stamp Gallery). This aspect of human nature is essential to understanding how people will choose to interact with works of their time. "A man hears what he wants to hear / And disregards the rest." (Simon)

Conclusion: Cultural Niches with a Universal Cultural Platform

The computers in which memes live are human brains. Time is possibly a more important limiting factor than storage space, and it is the subject of substantial competition. The human mind, and the body that it controls cannot do more than one or a few things at once. If a meme is to dominate the attention of a human brain, it must do so at the expense of `rival' memes" (Dawkins). When Richard Dawkins coined the phrase "meme" he did so without realizing just how universal that term would become. Now technology has allowed people to alter the specific meaning of interesting moments within creative works to the context in which the user is currently operating in a while retaining the soundbite pithiness that came from the original. However, there is also a natural tendency for a meme to lose the perceived novelty it once held whether by how individuals were using it or by simple competition. However, as has already noted time being sunk into a recreation of all varieties is likely to increase, and with its attention and effort spent on works will increase per person. The relevance of increased attention cannot be understated as the nature of online media consumption is exponential. Or to use Malcolm Gladwell's summary of his book on this subject "Ideas and products and messages and behaviors spread just like viruses do"(Gladwell). His examples for his point as the book was published at the turn of the millennia would not have included the unusual incident that was Gangnam style. The content of the video was a fairly silly flirtatious song with lines like "sexy lady" so there was nothing truly extraordinary about the song except that it was at the right place at the right time on YouTube. Even now comments a day old traffic more than two hundred views (YouTube). Its growth rate increased exponentially and explosively only being limited by the viewers of YouTube itself. This nature curbs itself for there are limits on the human attention span, and so just so many ideas will become universal for the human species. This trend of competition is demonstrated in older mediums such as television where the hour to show ratio has been drastically reduced (Wired). In conclusion, more time will be available to the masses for the consumption and production of works because of automation and because of this standards will be changed from the accessible (or the simple) to the universal (what connects to deeper human meaning) for what becomes part of the universal human culture. Pieces like Gangnam style will likely be an exception rather than the norm in the future.

Works Cited

Arbesman, Samuel. " Television Show Longevity by Network" *Wired*, www.wired.com/2012/03/television-show-longevity-by-network/. Accessed 11 April 2017.

"Average amount of time spent on leisure and sports by U.S. civilian population from 2009 to 2015 (hours per day)"*Statistica*, https://www.statista.com/statistics/189498/daily-average-time-spent-on-sports-and-leisure-in-the-us/. Accessed 10 April 2017.

Camus, Albert. *The Myth of Sisyphus and Other Essays* Translated by Justin O'Brien, Hamish Hamilton, 1955.

Dawkins, Richard. *The Selfish Gene*. Oxford University Press, 1976.

George, Katy. Interview by Nora Young. "Automation for the people?." *Spark*, CBC, 26

Mar. 2017

www.cbc.ca/radio/spark/350-disappearing-trades-automation-and-more-1.4033027/automation-for-the-people-1.4033044

Gladwell, Malcolm. *The Tipping Point*. Back Bay Books, 2000.

Heath, Chip, and Chris Bell and Emily Steinberg. "Emotional Selection in Memes: The Case of Urban Legends" *Journal of Personality and Social Psychology,* 2001, pp. 1024-1041.

Jae-sang, Park. "PSY - GANGNAM STYLE(강남스타일) M/V." *YouTube*, uploaded by officialpsy, 15 July 2012, www.youtube.com/watch?v=9bZkp7q19f0.

J. Howard Miller. We Can Do It. 1942, printed poster, National Archives, Washington, D.C..

Saad, Lydia. "The "40-Hour" Workweek Is Actually Longer -- by Seven Hours" *Gallup*,

www.gallup.com/poll/175286/hour-workweek-actually-longer-seven-hours.aspx. Accessed 10 April 2017.

Simon, Paul. *The Boxer.* 1698

"The Cross Platform Report: A Look Across Screens" *nielsen*, 6 Oct.

2013,www.nielsen.com/us/en/insights/reports/2013/the-cross-platform-report--a-look-across-screens.html. Accessed 10 April 2017

Thompson, Derek. "A World Without Work." *The Atlantic*, July/August 2015.

"Vacation Leave" *DEPARTMENT OF LABOR*,

2014,www.dol.gov/general/topic/workhours/vacation_leave. Accessed 10 April 2017.

"Women support war effort" *U.S.stampgallery*,

www.usstampgallery.com/view.php?id=1352aaaa8d4396c687fbde59ce0e09035b7c418a. Accessed 10 April 2017.

Chapter 7. Wage Inequality: To What Extent do the Wages of Executives Reflect Their Contribution to Society?

Introduction

Following the financial crisis of 2008, corporate executives found themselves under greater scrutiny than ever before. Until then, executives were given free-reign with little to no oversight. So long as their results pleased their shareholders, nobody thought to follow the paper-trail of how the results were achieved, and if anyone did, they often found themselves silenced in their quest for truth. But eventually all sins come to light, and this was indeed the case for the world's biggest investment banks. Forensic accountants and journalists pored over incriminating documents which presented evidence of fraud and repackaged, subprime loans; however, these were not the only crimes exposed.

When those responsible for the crisis were brought to the U.S. House of Representatives for questioning, it was revealed that many executives were still being paid, even after their companies had gone bankrupt. As Richard Fuld, the CEO of Lehman Brothers was famously asked: "Your company is now bankrupt, our economy is in crisis, but you get to keep $480 million. Is this fair (Bankruptcy)?" According to a survey by the Stanford School of Business, only 16% of Americans would defend this decision. (Donatello)

With an increasingly shrinking middle class, the gap between the pay of executives and the average worker has never been more relevant. How is it that two people can work for the same amount of time, and yet one emerges with hundreds of times the other's wages? However, this inequity is the basis of a market economy: all hands are not made equal, and some people are more efficient and innovative than others, and thus better equipped to climb the social ladder to success. But when those at the top boast wages 2000 times that of the average worker, it becomes tough to justify their wages solely by "above-average capabilities."

Even Adam Smith, the father of the market-economy system, recognized that it takes more than pure talent to justify substantial wage gaps. While The Wealth of Nations is considered the quintessential work which encourages greed and political awareness, it also makes a case for why wage gaps should exist. In the Tenth chapter "Inequalities of Wages," Smith identifies five main factors behind wage inequity. Three of these will be discussed in the context of executive compensation: "the easiness and cheapness, or the difficulty and expense of learning [a trade]," "the probability or improbability of success [in a certain profession]" and "the constancy or inconstancy of employment" (Smith).

Tricks of the Trade

Before passing judgment, it is essential to discuss what executives do. If the job, in and of itself, calls for people to go above and beyond the average skill set to be successful, then they would be paid accordingly. After all, doctors are paid so handsomely not only because they go to school longer than the average person, but also because their profession requires a particular skill set to be successful.

The CEO's role, primarily, is to run the company. Shareholders set some benchmark which should be reached by the end of the year; so long as it is met, an executive can continue their tenure at the company. In the case of an investment bank, this benchmark would be a certain amount of revenue which would increase the value of their shares and make up for any business expenses incurred. There are many ways by which these benchmarks can be reached and, while some methods work better than others, the preferred method for most executives is social networking.

Many of the seemingly extravagant galas and conferences attended by CEOs are not purely social events. While there, a CEO must not only entertain his guests but also gather as much information as he can about the current market in addition to "insights" on future developments that could impact the attainment of his benchmark. Along with this, he must continue to network and ensure that significant investors - whether private or institutional - continue to invest in his company. In short, the CEO's job requires both social and academic intelligence, which are not always comorbid (Rainey). In fact, the difference between a mediocre executive and a talented one could translate into billions of dollars in missed revenue.

In the case of Exxon-Mobil, the employment of Lee Raymond was undoubtedly a success. Where the average oil company made a return of 205% on their investment, under Raymond's leadership, Exxon-Mobil made a 223% return, which translates to a premium of $16 billion (Reich).

With this in mind, it is almost shocking to discover that Raymond only received 4% of the revenue he generated for his company. Of course, that 4% translated to $400 million in compensation, but it is clear that Raymond went above and beyond the average executive, and in a reward-based system, it would only follow that he be paid above and beyond the average executive.

The average Fortune 500 executive only makes $10.8 million (Reich), which is a sharp contrast to media publications about executives earning billions of dollars annually. While society would consider this to be excessive, it is nothing in comparison to what executives in the top 10 companies make. Even in the top 20 companies, the median wage is $36 million (Reich). As mentioned before, in a reward-based system, it would make sense that someone who generates enough revenue for their company to be placed in the top 10 - let alone 5 - deserves "extra" compensation, and this is the rationale behind executive compensation. To make it big in venture capitalism, you can't be average; you must be extraordinary. Therefore, those who manage to achieve such feats should be compensated accordingly.

STRAIGHT TO THE SOURCE

It is clear that merely expecting people to go above and beyond without any immediate gratification can be trying, which is why many companies offer stock options to push their executives' ingenuity. The use of stock options has been widely successful, to the point that a study by MIT and Stanford researchers Frydman and Jenter found that stock incentives "...substantially strengthened the link between CEO wealth and... performance".

Following the 1970s, executive compensation became 'excessive,' and this rise is frequently attributed to the addition of stock options to compensation packages. Stock incentives allow executives to become shareholders in their own company, which means that "the typical executive stands to gain millions from improving firm performance" (Frydman), without even taking into account their regular salary. This form of compensation promotes corporate greed as executives tend to pursue ventures which will reap the most amount of money upfront, even though the cheapest way is not always the best way.

At the heart of the debate concerning executive compensation is corporate greed. Most tabloids have bemoaned an executive's purchase of his fifth private jet or private island, and it is when executives show off their generous endowments that people began to cry "greedy." However, isn't Adam Smith's market economy premised on the philosophy that "greed is good?" By weaponizing people's natural tendency to do what is in their best interest, companies get executives with powerful incentive to work hard and efficiently.

But when corporate greed gets out of hand, there can be disastrous results. In the case of Enron, fixation on stock options led to excessive risk-taking and creative accounting methods' which allowed executives to earn millions of dollars a week. Because compensation packages did not fall under US accounting laws, there was no mandate which forced executives to admit where the money came from. Stock options were meant to ensure executives were not too risk-averse, but their usage has created a culture in which high-risk ventures are more lucrative because the enormous reward blinds people to the severe risk. However, in the context of venture capitalism, it would make sense that the system would be skewed towards risk, especially when the company is in its infancy and the venture capitalism risk-reward system is at its most precarious.

REAP WHAT YOU SOW:

In "Inequalities of Wages," Smith claims that "the probability or improbability of success [in a certain profession]" and "the constancy or inconstancy of employment" should be taken into consideration when debating the merit of wage inequality. The basis of this argument is the main reason why many venture capitalists believe they are justified in making many times more than the average worker. After all, venture capitalism is one of the riskiest business ventures a person can tie their name to, which is why companies prefer to either have a highly experienced person at the helm or the very least, someone with high motivation to become successful very quickly.

By sitting atop a large, globally recognized or publicly traded company, an executive essentially ties their fate to their company's success. Much like the smuggler metaphor in "The Wealth of Nations, "when the [venture] succeeds [working as an executive] is likewise the most profitable," but it is also "the infallible road to bankruptcy" (Smith). While this may seem ridiculous, it has been demonstrated that an executive's failure has much more significant long-term ramifications than that of a working-class citizen.

If a company goes bankrupt, 70-90% of the time the executive is fired. Further, "only 12 percent of dismissed CEOs land comparable positions with other public companies (The Rationale…). If they do, "it is likely at a much smaller firm at a greatly reduced salary." (The Rationale) Even if the circumstances surrounding their company's bankruptcy were out of their control, many executives who lead failing companies find their names forever tarnished, often globally, in this era of social media. Because of this, an executive must not only work with the short-term in mind but also the long-term. It is entirely possible that an executive could go from being employed one day to unemployed the next and, all they would have is whatever remains of their last paycheck. However, an executive's nest egg is colossal relative to the average working class citizens'. While an executive might find it difficult to find work again, someone fired from McDonald's could find themselves unable to pay for essential amenities. The only time when this risk for the executive seems to be on-par with that of a working-class citizen is when a business venture is just-starting-out, which is why even the threat of moderate risk translates to an 18.4% wage increase for executives compared to better-established companies. (The Rational).

Conclusion

While many are quick to claim any wage gap 'excessive,' some solid arguments are supporting this wage inequity. Some executives do turn to illegal methods to reach their goals; however, many genuinely creative individuals go on to revolutionize the industry. Although risk-taking may be dangerous, it fosters innovation. Lowering compensation levels would cheapen the efforts of those who manage to make it to the top, and even stifle creativity. However, not every executive will take this venture seriously, so some caps must be placed to avert situations like the financial crisis in future.

One promising proposal is indexed stock options (ISO) which only allow compensation "to the extent that [executive's] performance exceeds the market" (Hall). In other words, industrial pioneers would have wages which reflect their contribution to society, while an executive who merely maintains a company's prosperity would make less. There would still be an incentive to work hard, as executives who follow the example of Raymond would also be compensated accordingly. Indexed options would be placed under review by law, so it would be difficult for a company to make a good case for their executive's pay-raise without good reason. Along with this, there should be a solid cap on how much executives of any level can make.

In 1993, the Revenue Reconciliation Act (RRA) was created to "[limit] the corporate tax deduction for executive compensation to $1 million per individual." (Balsam) However, it did not include compensation as tax-deductible, so executives naturally turned to stock-options to ensure they received a similar amount of pay. But with the combination of the RRA and ISOs, executive compensation could be capped without deterring too many people from taking risks. While greed is not always a good thing if it can be used for good, such that the sky is indeed the limit.

WORKS CITED

Balsam, Steven. "Limiting executive compensation: the case of CEOs hired after the imposition of 162(m)." N.p.

"Bankruptcy of Lehman Brothers." Wikipedia. Wikimedia Foundation, 08 Apr. 2017. Web. 04 Apr.

2017.

Donatiello, Nicholas and Larcker, David F. "Americans and CEO Pay: 2016 Public Perception Survey on CEO Compensation." Stanford School of Business; Rock Center for Corporate Governance. n.p., 2016.

Frydman, Carola and Jenter, Dirk. "CEO Compensation." NBER.. Issue 16585.

N.p. December 2010.

Hall, Brian J. and Murphy, Kevin J. "The Trouble With Stock Options." Journal of Economic Perspectives. Volume 17, Number 3. 2003. 49-70. Print.

Rainey, Don. "4 Skills CEOs Have That You Might Lack." Business Insider. Business Insider, 28 Sept. 2010. Web. 01 Apr. 2017.

Reich, Robert B. "CEOs deserve their Pay." Wall Street Journal. 14 September 2007. pp. A13

Smith, Adams. "Chapter 10 Part 1: Of Wages and Profit in the different employments of Labour and Stock." The Wealth of Nations. N.p.:n.p., 1904. 101-120. Print/

"The Rationale behind CEO Compensation." Arizona State University: W.P. Carey School of Business Research and Ideas. 14 March 2013.

Chapter 8. To What Extent Does Financial Incentives Affect Workers' Quality of Workforce?

Introduction

Before the scientific researches came out, many companies were paying their workers bonuses and additional salary to motivate them. However, as this continued, companies slowly ran out of money, and all of those workers, who did not receive any financial motivation, decided to leave their businesses. According to Nixon's speech, it says that the four element of productivity includes: "Investment in new technology, job training, good management, and high employee motivation" (Nixon). It is true that high employee motivation is vital to increase the productivity of these workers, but in many cases, extrinsic motivations are seemed to be ineffective. Although many businesses believe in the ideology of Adam Smith, where he talks about in his The Wealth of Nations that higher wage will attract workforce to the fields that are "disagreeable [...], difficult [...], and inconstant" (Smith), the researches show that this "higher wage" does not improve the quality of the workforce.

According to "Why Incentive Plans Cannot Work" written by Harvard Business Review, these rewards "do not create a lasting commitment" (Harvard). The impacts that are given by the extrinsic motivation are all known to be temporary, and it does not motivate workers to perform better. To create a sustainable business with motivated employees, it is essential to know what kind of motivations can increase productivity. In "Small Business: Causes of Bankruptcy" written by Don Bradley III and Chris Cowdery, professors at the University of Central Arkansas, they talk about how "28% of small business went bankrupt because of financing" (Bradley III). This proves that companies, especially small businesses, often do not have enough finance to sustain their business. While capital is essential to keep businesses running, these small businesses cannot afford to finance all of their capitals to motivate workers extrinsically. If these companies can find a way to motivate their employees, without the help of financially driving them, these companies can become the next blue-chip company. Adam Smith believed that the rise of new enterprises would create competition in the market, thus creating more innovation and prevent monopoly of specific products. To create this financially-fostering environment that Adam Smith envisioned, all of these companies must learn to implement intrinsic motivation and publicly acknowledgment.

    Richard M. Ryan, the professor at the University of Rochester, defines intrinsic motivation as "the doing of an activity for its inherent satisfactions rather than [...] because of external prods, pressures, or rewards" (Ryan). Workers who are intrinsically motivated tend to be more creative with their tasks, and have higher productivity than of their extrinsic counterparts. Oppositions often claim that "behavior can be conditioned and shaped [...] through the pattern of stimulus-response-reinforcement" (Skinner); therefore, by rewarding the prominent workers with financial motivation, it will encourage these workers to continue with their high level of productivity. However, Roland Benabou, a researcher at Princeton University, writes in his scholarly article "Intrinsic and Extrinsic Motivation," that "rewards are positive short-term reinforcers" (Benabou) and this will not continue to improve the quality of the workforce.

Despite the traditional belief of businesses, this paper argues that companies should look to encourage their workforce by intrinsic motivations or publicly to acknowledge their work, rather than paying bonuses or increase in salary. The two most important issues of financial incentives are the workers' expectation to be rewarded and limitation of innovation.

Worker's Expectation: The Implication of Being Rewarded Continuously

One of the most detrimental effects of financially rewarding outstanding workers is that it creates a dangerous assumption that they will always be paid for their work. The problem with this expectation is that if they are not rewarded because businesses' lack of finance, they will most likely quit their job or become unmotivated to do their work. Not only that but financially satisfying an individual can create a severe competition among the employees in the workforce, therefore, decreasing productivity.

In a research conducted by Lalin Anik and Lara Aknin, the Professors of Business and Psychology for Duke University and Simon Fraser University demonstrates that "rewarding individual employees can produce adverse outcomes by eroding workplace cohesion" (Anik). If one particular person is rewarded with their work, other co-workers, who also want to be paid, would not want to cooperate with that individual. This is mainly because the colleagues, who helped that person to achieve that goal, are not rewarded with the amount of work that they have done. It is dangerous for companies to pay all of their workers every time they get a quality job done. With intrinsic motivation and public acknowledgment, companies can reward their workers without financially risking their profits and prevent dispute among their workers.

Secondly, financial incentives will significantly decrease the productivity of the workforce because owners and managers will expect better results from these workers. If these workers are not able to reach the same amount of productivity as before, companies will often choose to fire that person or pressure them to create this amount of productivity. However, companies need to recognize that workers are not driven by the managers' expectations. In a research done by Anthony Nyberg and Jenna Pieper, the professors of University of South Carolina and University of Nebraska- Lincoln, it states that bonuses are often "payment used to recognize past performance", but that does not mean their "productivity [... will improve] as their wages increase" (Nyberg). There are seems to be no correlation between some bonuses given and the productivity of the workers in most cases. Employees are often motivated by their will to do their work, rather than how much they are paid to do so.

    In "Project Innovation," researchers looked at the effects that extrinsic and intrinsic motivation had on teachers' class performances. In this research, teachers were given a choice to teach a subject that they are passionate in or to teach a subject that paid them more. By comparing these two results, researchers were able to discover that teachers who chose the topic that they are passionate about, "[led] students to [learn] more easily and speedily, persevere in their studies and be more successful" (Innovation). This shows that those who are intrinsically motivated, such as teaching a class because of their passion, will both increase the productivity of the students and teachers. Intrinsic motivation does not risk any financial instability, and still, provide higher productivity of the workforce.

   However, the opposition claims that there are some cases where extrinsic motivation does work to improve the quality of the workforce. According to the scholarly article, "Extrinsic Motivation as Correlates of Work Attitude of the Nigerian Police Force: Implications for Counseling", written by Sylvester Nosakhare, Professor for Department of Educational Psychology at University of Benin, it states that "promotion and enhanced salary income can effectively promote work attitude of the Nigeria police". Although this example provides a credible source, police officers often work in a different environment than companies. If companies are not innovative or do not provide reliable services, they will often be out of business. In the other hand, police forces are not "put out of business" because they are part of the public service. No matter how bad their services are, they cannot be replaced by another service.

   In conclusion, financial incentives create a dangerous assumption for both the employers and the employee. This expectation can often jeopardize the company's finances, and disrupt its workers.

LIMITATION OF INNOVATION: THE IMPLICATION OF APPROVED METHOD OF WORK

Another issue with extrinsic motivation is that there is no innovation among the workforce because financial incentives set up the anticipation of what method of work will be approved. When one employee is rewarded with extrinsic motivation for what they have done, other workers will try to do the same action to get the same. This will ultimately cause conformity among the workforce, thus decreasing the quality of the workforce.

     Creativity is not created by financial motivation, but rather from the employees' will to be innovative. According to Teresa Amabile and Steve Kramer, in their article, "What Doesn't Motivate Creativity Can Kill It," extrinsic motivation can "constantly [show the workers what] exact rewards will follow from which actions." They were able to come to this conclusion by comparing two groups who were motivated extrinsically and intrinsically. Those who were extrinsically driven by financial incentives did significantly worse than those who were intrinsically excited because the amount of money cannot influence how creative a worker can be. By instead being motivated by their curiosity, it costs less to drive them and increase productivity.

     Unfortunately, with current businesses' traditional belief, financial incentives motivate workers to repeat the action that rewarded individual did, rather than creating their innovative methods. With this, there will be no room for innovation, and the workers' productivity will go down. To create the environment that Adam Smith suggests in his The Wealth of Nations, innovation is essential to stimulate competition among the market. With financial incentives restricting the creativity of workers, this environment cannot be created.

However, opposition states that extrinsic motivation does increase the productivity of the construction workers. In "Motivating Workers in Construction," written by Jason E. Barg and Rajeev Ruparathna, professors at Faculty of Applied Science, they write that providing additional bonuses for these workers can be "more rewarding and satisfying to workers," thus allowing them to work harder (Barg). Although this may true for uncomplicated labors that construction workers need to do, such as repetitive movement of building a foundation, this is not true for businesses. Businesses need innovation and creativity to profit, rather than repeating what other workers are doing. This shows that only a few workforces that do not require creativity can benefit from financial incentives.

Recommendation

It is shown that many businesses are trying to encourage their workers by providing bonuses and additional salary. However, several types of research conclude that financial incentives decrease the quality of workforces. By giving extrinsic motivation, it creates an unrealistic expectation that all workers are going to be rewarded with their achievements. Rather than relying on financial motives, these workers should be paid by being acknowledged publicly.

In Adam Smith's The Wealth of Nations, he states that "public admiration which attends upon such distinguished abilities, always makes a part of their reward" (Smith). This means that by giving these prominent figures a public appreciation, such as publicly recognizing their work, it will encourage these workers to have high productivity and quality of work. Employees will want to perform better out of their will, rather than always being driven by bonuses and increased salary.

According to Mark McGuinness, the author of Motivation for Creative People, he states that "people will be most creative when they feel motivated primarily by the interest, satisfaction, and challenge of the work itself — not by external pressures." When employees are driven by their will, this is when their creativity begins to spark. If extrinsic motivation, such as bonuses, are introduced, it reduces workers' self-motivation and converts it to external motivation. For creativity to be created, these workers should continue to do something out of their will.

A limitation of this solution is it is difficult to distinguish when companies can use financial incentives. As stated by the opposition, the police force and the construction workers were primarily motivated by the financial incentives that their managers have promised. To reward an individual by publicly acknowledging them, few conditions must be taken in place. First of all, these workers should not be financially suffering because they do not receive bonuses anymore. If they cannot afford to fulfill their basic needs, they will most likely not favor the public acknowledgment rather than financial incentives. Secondly, with essential labors that include repetitive movements, extrinsic motivation should be the primary driving force of these workers.

  To eliminate the external pressure and conformity in the workplace, people should not be motivated by bonuses or higher salary, but rather from public acknowledgment. This will mostly drive them to continue with their action out of their will, which allows their determination to heighten and creativity to flow. To create a better financial market and create the financially-fostering environment that Adam Smith visualized, companies should stop using financial incentives to motivate workers, but instead, create intrinsic motivations to drive them.

WORKS CITED

Akhtar, Sajjad Hayat, et al. "Effectiveness of Extrinsic Motivation in the Teaching of English Language in government girls high schools of Khyber Pakhtunkhwa, Pakistan." *Resource Center*, Sept. 2015, go.galegroup.com/ps/i.do?p=LitRC&sw=w&u=edmo88552&v=2.1&it=r&id=GALE%7CA433739822&asid=efa4eab88eca203598d2e34f4c4f62d7

Amabile, Teresa., Kramer, Steve. "What Doesn't Motivate Creativity Can Kill It" *Harvard Business Review*, April 25, 2012, https://hbr.org/2012/04/balancing-the-four-factors-tha-1

Anik, Lalin. Aknin, Lara. "Prosocial Bonuses Increase Employee Satisfaction and Team Performance" *Plos One,* September 18, 2013, http://journals.plos.org/plosone/article?id=10.1371/journal.pone.0075509

Barg, Jason E., Ruparathna, Rajeev., Mendis, Daylath., Hewage, Kasun N. "Motivating Workers in Construction" *Journal of Construction Engineering*, July 9th 2014 https://www.hindawi.com/journals/jcen/2014/703084/

Benabou Roland., Triole Jean. "Intrinsic and Extrinsic Motivation" *Princeton University*, January 2003, https://www.princeton.edu/~rbenabou/papers/RES2003.pdf

Kohn, Alfied. "Why Incentive Plans Cannot Work" *Harvard Business Review*, September 1993, https://hbr.org/1993/09/why-incentive-plans-cannot-work

Bradley III, Don B., Cowdery Chris. "Small Business: Causes of Bankruptcy" *University of Central Arkansas,* August 2004 "https://pdfs.semanticscholar.org/0fc2/c3c3b4bd056d028bb0204535821c728d2af3.pdf

Celikoz, Nadir. "Basic factors that affect general academic motivation levels of candidate preschool teachers." *Opposing Viewpoints in Context,* October 2010, link.galegroup.com/apps/doc/A239813830/OVIC?u=edmo88552&xid=082a744e.

Eisenberger, Robert., Shanock, Linda. "Rewards, Intrinsic Motivation, and Creativity: A Case Study of Conceptual and Methodological Isolation" *Creativity Research Journal,* 2003, http://kids-n-music.com/Research/Creativity_and_Rewards.pdf

Igun, Sylvester Nosakhare. "Extrinsic motivation as correlates of work attitude of the Nigerian police for: implications for counseling" *Opposing Viewpoints in Context*, December 2008, link.galegroup.com/apps/doc/A190331800/OVIC?u=edmo88552&xid=7625e98b.

Maximino, Martin. "Pay-for-Performance, Merit Pay, Bonuses and Worker Productivity: Research Roundup" *Journalist's Resource,* April 3, 2014, https://journalistsresource.org/studies/economics/workers/wages-gifts-worker-productivity

McGuinness, Mark. "What Motivation Does to Your Creativity" *The Creative Pathfinder,* March 2012, http://lateralaction.com/motivation-creativity/

Morris, Edward K., Nathaniel G. Smith, and Deborah E. Altus. "B. F. Skinner's Contributions to Applied Behavior Analysis." *The Behavior Analyst* 28.2 (2005): 99–131. Print. https://www.ncbi.nlm.nih.gov/pmc/articles/PMC2755377/

Ryan, Richard M., Deci, Edward L. "Intrinsic and Extrinsic Motivations: Classic Definitions and New Directions" *University of Rochester,* July 2000, https://mmrg.pbworks.com/f/Ryan,+Deci+00.pdf

Zhao, Lili. "The influence of learners' motivation and attitudes on second language teaching." *Literature Resource Center,* Nov. 2015, go.galegroup.com/ps/i.do?p=LitRC&sw=w&u=edmo88552&v=2.1&it=r&id=GALE%7CA446637390&asid=833124ad7d8d2ca9993d11106d8e8774.

Chapter 9. Environmental Impact of Integrating Endangered Cultures into Modern Society

The Earth is an unbelievably expansive place. With its landmass covering 149,000,000km square, the Earth is home to diverse cultures and environments.("Earth physical characteristics tables" 1) The planet is the home to hundreds of different landscapes and thousands of unique upbringings that shape the lifestyles people lead. Distressingly though, the biodiversity and the cultural diversity of the globe are at risk.("Climate change: How do we know?" 1) A likely future for society will involve somehow integrating the endangered cultures with the hope of helping them retain their religion, and hopefully end up protecting the environment. To what extent should endangered cultures be integrated into society?

To begin, if we as a society were to physically integrate indigenous people into our community and cities, they would start producing as much carbon emissions as we do because of modern lifestyles and new infrastructure. This can be inferred by comparing CO2e (carbon dioxide equivalent) emissions of city life and CO2e of traditional ways of life. In Canada on average, we produce 20.3 tonnes per capita, ("Greenhouse Gas (GHG) Emissions" 1) which is substantial compared to "[...] two tonnes per person as it is currently in Brazil or the Dominican Republic. Emissions from most indigenous peoples are even lower and are amongst the lowest in the world."(Leahy 1). Living in cities and living urban lifestyles will lead them to contribute more to emissions than if they didn't integrate into cities.

Continuing with that, it is also important to consider the infrastructure we would need to build to support more people living in cities. The process of collecting resources, transporting them, and constructing them is a large contributor to global CO2e emissions. "[...] This gives the embodied energy of the development as 650 Kgs CO2e per square meter. That is 65 tonnes CO2e for a 100m2 flat."("Carbon Footprint of Building Construction" 1) Considering the thousands of homes that would need to be built to support new residences, that is a significant amount of greenhouse gases. At the same time, it is important to note that infrastructure isn't a continuous contribution to CO2e, as it's carbon footprint diminishes over time. For example, a house built 30 years ago has contributed less CO2e per year than a home built today. Overall though, integrating endangered cultures into modern society will increase the global CO2e emissions and in turn negatively impact the environment.

  A huge benefit to socially integrating endangered cultures into modern society would be the knowledge they could teach us. Indigenous peoples around the world possess a deep understanding of their local environments, which can help researchers pinpoint what they need to focus on in their research. 6 "Local knowledge may make it possible to survey and map in a few days what would otherwise take months"(Johannes 2). It is obvious on how vital this could be. Adding on, the extensive knowledge of indigenous populations applies to other factors such as the makeup of the ecosystem. For example, they might depend on a species to hunt for food. If the species were negatively impacted, it could be inferred that they either know about it or involved, by either trying to negate or add to the negative impact.(Guevara 4) Additionally, the perspective indigenous populations hold is highly regarded because of reasons above. "Some authors suggest that conservation strategies that consider indigenous ecological knowledge, management practices, and customary sea tenure institutions have a higher rate of local acceptance and, consequently, greater conservation value"(Cinner 2). It is also important to recognize that indigenous knowledge isn't best. Put simply by a native farmer in Tanzania when interviewed, "If indigenous knowledge is so good, why is my farm so poor?"(Briggs 3). It is wrong to assume that indigenous populations have the answer to everything, but even if only half of what we could learn applies to what we need to know it would just still be worth it. Overall the knowledge and experiences from various groups on how to protect the environment we could collectively gain by integrating endangered cultures have a positive impact on the environment.

    Our societies would impact the environment and resource development, and negate problems that arise if they were integrated and harmonized. In some cases, the indigenous people will negatively impact the environment. A good example would be the native population in the Republic of Panama.(Guevara 2) Around the turn of the century, coral reef degradation started to become a huge problem and researchers found that it was linked to the rapidly increasing population, and local developments. "We measured 20 km of a seawall built with mined reef corals (16,000 m3) and an increase in island surface area of 6.23 ha caused by coral landfilling."(Guevara 2). The indigenous people worked with researchers and later set up nature reserves to protect the coral reefs. This shows that working together and integrating our societies can positively impact the environment. At the same time, we can be very much in the wrong when it comes to protecting it. "To reduce plastic waste and negative effects, recycling programs have been implemented in many parts of the United States, but remain underutilized. [...] Immense quantities of plastic are also sent to the developing world together with e-waste, where "recycling" frequently involves open-air burning."(Stephens 1) Open-air burnings of plastic are incredibly toxic to the environment. Our own "solutions," don't solve much. Overall it is essential that moving forward we all learn from each other to solve a problem and benefit as a whole better.

      In brief, we should integrate endangered cultures to some extent into modern society. The environment would be negatively impacted by physically incorporating indigenous peoples into society. It will lead to more people producing significant amounts of CO2e, which in turn damages the environment. On the other hand, if we socially integrate we can learn new things about ecosystems and how to better protect it. Integrating allows us to also learn from each other's mistakes. Moving forward as a society, it is essential to work together with all peoples to reach a brighter future for everyone and the planet.

Works Cited

Briggs, J. "The use of indigenous knowledge in development: problems and challenges". *University of Glasgow,* p.1-5, 2005.
eprints.gla.ac.uk/1094/1/JBriggs_eprint1094.pdf.
"Carbon Footprint of Building Construction". *green ration book,* www.greenrationbook.org.uk/resources/footprints-building-construction/.

Cinner, Joshua. "Integrating customary management into marine conservation". *Australian Research*

> *Council Centre of Excellence,* p.1-4, westernsolomons.uib.no/docs/Aswani,%20Shankar/Cinner%20and%20Aswani%20(2007)%20Integrating%20customary%20management%20into%20marine%20conservation%20(review).pdf.

"Climate change: How do we know?". *Nasa,* climate.nasa.gov/evidence/.

"Earth physical characteristics tables". *Wikipedia.* May 30, 2016.

> en.wikipedia.org/wiki/Earth_physical_characteristics_tables.

"Greenhouse Gas (GHG) Emissions" *The Conference Board of Canada,*

> www.conferenceboard.ca/hcp/details/environment/greenhouse-gas-emissions.aspx.

Guevara, Carlos. "Natural Disturbances and Mining of Panamanian Coral Reefs by Indigenous

People."

Conservation Biology, vol.17, no.5, pp.2-4. October 2003, stri.si.edu/sites/publications/PDFs/2003_KunaYala_Guzman.pdf.

Johannes, R.E. "Integrating Traditional Ecological Knowledge and Management with

Environmental Impact Assessment". *DLIST,* p.1-3, www.dlist.org/sites/default/files/doclib/indigenous%20knowledge%20and%20eia.pdf.

Leahy, Stephen. "Indigenous Peoples Can Show the Path to Low-Carbon Living If Their Land

Rights Are Recognized". *National Geographic,* April 4, 2012. voices.nationalgeographic.com/2012/04/04/indigenous-peoples-can-show-the-path-to-low-carbon-living-if-their-land-rights-are-recognized/.

"List of countries by carbon dioxide emissions per capita". *Wikipedia,* October 20, 2016.

en.wikipedia.org/wiki/List_of_countries_by_carbon_dioxide_emissions_ per_capita.

Stephens, Rachael. "Plastics, human health and environmental impacts: The road ahead".

Journalist's Resource,
journalistsresource.org/studies/environment/polluti
on-environment/plastics-environmental-health-
literature-review.

"The Environmental & Cultural Disintegration of Africa". *African Conservancy,*

> www.africanconservancy.org/about/documents/Pro
> blem_1206.pdf.

Wade, Davis. "Dreams from endangered cultures". *Ted,* Feb 2003.

> www.ted.com/talks/wade_davis_on_endangered_cu
> ltures.

Chapter 10. Economic Impact of Endangered Culture Integration

The integration of endangered cultures offers new perspectives and traditions to be integrated into society. While this aspect is positive, it is unwise to overlook the potential repercussion of removing these niche groups, as each contains untainted values, customs, and traditions worth cherishing. Isolated cultural groups allow individuals to create lifestyles and economies best suited to their environment, without the interference of outside or national law. If integrated, these external views could increase perspective in workplaces, but remove the previously established local markets from existence, with no chance of return. The question remains; it economically correct to integrate endangered cultures into society?

If integrated, the previous economies of cultural groups would almost certainly be removed, for example, the hunting economy of the Canadian Inuit. As described by Sarah Bonesteel in her paper describing the cultural impact on Nunavut governmental policy, this group of native Canadians has an economy based around hunting seals and the availability of the limited resources in the northern arctic environment. (1) These practices, while subsistent, allow local groups to make use of an otherwise untapped economic engine, as well as tourism. By being left alone, otherwise illegal practices, such as hunting, allow groups to generate revenue. If integrated, this source would remain barred from use as national laws forbid the shooting of, in most circumstances, the animals killed by many native groups. Oppositely, the removal of indigenous or endangered cultures from rural areas allows access to resource extraction on the site. For example, as stated in Finer et al.'s article about western amazon oil and gas distribution, many of the 688 000 km2 of oil and gas fields in the Amazon are home of indigenous tribes. (Finer) Naturally, access to oil and other resources, such as Amazon timber would be a significant economic benefit of cultural integration, especially for only the cost of comparatively insignificant local economies. However, the economic impacts of the citizen's change of lifestyle must remain an important consideration.

      An alternative lifestyle change for displaced cultural groups could be integration in workplaces in cities. As stated by Marlene Fine in her paper on workplace cultural diversity, A mix of cultures can significantly increase productivity. (487) Especially in the case of endangered cultures, a vast diversity delta causes problems to be viewed from more angles, allowing them to be solved more quickly and efficiently. Additionally, as described by Alesina and La Ferrara in their analysis on the economic impact of ethnic diversity, racial diversity causes people to think differently by exposure alone. (2) In consequence to enrichment, however, the disparity of language and customs can also slow communication, meaning that unless the cultural integration is encompassing, businesses could instead lose productivity more than enough to offset the additional efficiency. In stating this, it is important to remember that the relocation/homogenization of a population is not inherently free, and the legal costs of the ordeal would, more than likely, leave the venture unfeasible economically.

Endangered cultures can also economically affect populations indirectly, such as in the form of tax-funded government funding for aboriginal groups. In many cases, employment in indigenous communities is significantly lower than the general population, compensated for by outside assistance. Moving forward, this cost is only projected to increase. As described by James Ford in his article about the effects of climate change on Inuit populations, many environmentally based economic practices are no longer viable due to global temperature change. ("dangerous climate change" 3) Logically, this could Increase needed funding, since remaining industries largely comprise of administration. Also, the rapid growth of indigenous communities far surpasses the general population, leading to higher comparative costs independent of the previously stated issues. While is likely costs will rise overall, the opposite could also be true. As Ford states in another article, the temperature increase could instead provide more economic opportunities, such as clearing ice for durations long enough for fisheries in the region to be profitable. (et al., "climate change policy" 180) Overall, however integration of groups into mainstream society would increase employment and decrease spending, leading to a net economic benefit.

Overall, the integration of endangered cultural groups is a split economic issue. While cultural diversity can allow for a more extensive variety of businesses, opinions and perspectives, the sustenance of specifically indigenous cultures consume many resources, both economically and in the form of land. Within-population centers, however, diversity acts primarily as a beneficiary, so long as it avoids Total assimilation. The most economically ideal extent to which endangered cultures should be preserved would be the integration of them in population centers while keeping their values and ideas. This would allow cultural enrichment to be maintained and appreciated by citizens in closer communities, as well as open new space for economic ventures and infrastructure development. So long as the transitional cost is low enough, both diversity and prosperity can be maintained and appreciated with economic benefit.

OTHER INFORMATION AND IMPLICATIONS

Cultures forming the minority in a country, or globally, as well as cultures whose traditions, languages, and way of life are disappearing faster than their members are, can both be classified as endangered. These cultures are often under threat of marginalization in politics, and so may choose to remain secluded and self-determining. However, with the rise of globalization, endangered cultures can be left with little choice on whether to integrate into modern society. The question then occurs of how much, and in what way the cultures should be integrated.

Integrating endangered cultures politically with more dominating cultures in their region can cause the larger system to overlook the specific concerns of the endangered culture. Having unique concerns, and a different set of values from mainstream culture, the endangered culture runs the risk, with integration, of having its voice go unheard. It is not uncommon for national governments to the ignore the concerns of minority cultures within their country, in favour of pursuing their own goals. The native peoples of the United States and in Canada for example, frequently are challenged by the government for their rights to land or political self-determination. In the 1960's, the Native Americans of Alaska were only slowly beginning to conform to Western cultural expectations, and a series of conflicts between them and the Alaskan government, initiated by a dispute over the rights of the Native people to their traditional land, climaxed with the Native people legally impeding construction of the Alaska Pipeline in 1968. In a position of political weakness, the United States Congress created the Alaska Native Claims Settlement Act (ANCSA)

In 1971 aiming to integrate the Native people into modern American life, and move them away from traditional subsistence and communal living towards a culture of private economic enterprise, more able to survive independently among larger contemporary economic forces. However, in doing so, the government moved from ignoring the importance of land to the Native people, to ignoring the emphasis they placed on their traditional societal structure, and political self-determination. By the end of the twentieth century, the economic, health, and education problems of the Native people continued. In 1992 though only 6.8% of all Alaskan families lived on an income below the poverty line, 21.5 % of Alaska Native families did. Many Alaskan Natives strove to re-establish traditional tribal government, and regain their sovereignty. Integrating the Native people to such a complete extent into the Modern american society had lasting negative consequences on the Native population.

Similar struggles are occurring currently; Native people of the Tsleil-Waututh nation in British Columbia began a court case against the Harper government in October of 2016 after feeling the government had not adequately consulted them in approval of the Kinder Morgan Trans Mountain pipeline expansion. The Tsleil-Waututh nation takes pride in being environmental stewards, and fears the carbon emissions, and possible oil spills the pipeline could cause, and the effects both could have on their culture.

Global political goals can often stand in opposition to local goals, especially those designed to help endangered cultures. Endangered cultures hold less world power than large and advanced countries, especially as the United States, which often exercise global political hegemony. So action taken to meet the needs of people in endangered cultures can be easily squashed by the much larger global players. In South Africa, for example, after the fall of the Apartheid regime in 1994 implemented the Reconstruction and Development Programme, a "coherent socio-economic policy framework" to rebuild an integrated country. This plan would improve the lives of minority cultures in South Africa, such as the Bantu, Khoisan, Malay, Griqua, or San peoples, who had been subject to horrendous oppression under the Apartheid regime. However, on grounds of its unstable economic strategy various African as well as International banks disapproved of the programme. Additionally, the RDP showed direct objection to the policies of International financial institutions. These institutions are necessary in South Africa, and loss of their support could result in capital flight, and so impair South

Africa's economy. The RDP was implemented in 1994, and however seemed successful in South Africa, with poverty rates among Africans dropping from an astronomical 71% in 1993 to 57% in 2008. A programme that had been so close to extinction under threat by global political powers, had ended up providing much-needed care for vulnerable peoples in South Africa. This demonstrates the negative effect the large negative impact integration into global politics can have on those vulnerable, endangered cultures.

Similar struggles are occurring currently; Native people of the Tsleil-Waututh nation in British Columbia began a court case against the Harper government in October of 2016 after feeling the government had not adequately consulted them in approval of the Kinder Morgan Trans Mountain pipeline expansion (McSheffrey). The Tsleil-Waututh nation takes pride in being environmental stewards, and fears the carbon emissions, and possible oil spills the pipeline could cause, and the effects both could have on their culture (Lo).

In being integrated into modern politics, endangered cultures run the risk of being ignored, but they may also have the new opportunity to be heard on a larger scale than when they remain isolated. Being present in global politics can create the opportunity for endangered cultures to speak out on issues that affect them, and garner extensive support. The Paris Agreement created during the 2015 climate talks was signed by 195 countries, and specifically mentions the need to consider the "rights of indigenous peoples, local communities, migrants, children, persons with disabilities and people in vulnerable situations" when taking action to combat climate change.

The theme of protecting vulnerable populations from the effects of climate change was continued from the Paris talks through those in Marrakech in 2016, held as the Paris Agreement was entered into force. The indigenous Kichwa people of Ecuador spoke in Marrakech on the direct impacts climate change was having on them, and accentuated the appeals of indigenous peoples to receive government support in combating climate change.

Though it remains to be seen if the promises to endangered cultures in the Paris Agreement will be kept, the addressing of the issue indicates the presence of the voices of endangered cultures in global politics.

Global political pressures can be used to force a country to change in ways that protect endangered cultures. With Myanmar's chairmanship of the Association of Southeast Asian Nations (ASEAN) in the 2014 regional groupings being conditional on it putting an end to its "abuses in ethnic conflict areas", and other human-rights centred criteria. The political benefits this would have for Myanmar pressures it to minimize the human rights violations that are so frequent in its borders, which would protect endangered cultures under threat of the government's violent military practices. This would include the Karen people, who have been waging an ongoing civil war for over sixty years to gain ethnic sovereignty. The Rohingya people, a muslim minority, who are denied citizenship by the Myanmar government would be protected by these actions from the violence they face through restrictions in their legal rights.

WORKS CITED

Alesina, Alberto. La Ferrara, Eliana. "Ethnic Diversity and Economic Performance".
dash.harvard.edu/bitstream/handle/1/4553005/alesinassrn_ethnicdiversity.pdf?sequence=2.
December, 2003.

Bonesteel, Sarah. "Use of Traditional Inuit Culture in the Policies and Organization of the Government of Nunavut".www.inuitoralityconference.com/art/Bonesteel.pdf. Paris, 2006.

Fine, Marlene G. "Cultural Diversity in the Workplace: The State of the Field".
www.researchgate.net/profile/Marlene_Fine/publication/258153893_Cultural_Diversity_in_the_Workplace_The_State_of_the_Field/links/56d864f108aebe4638b7c6fa.pdf. October, 1996.

Finer, Matt. Jenkins, Clinton N. Pimm, Stuart L. Keane, Brian. Ross, Carl. PLOS ONE. "Oil and Gas Projects in the Western Amazon: Threats to Wilderness, Biodiversity, and Indigenous Peoples".
journals.plos.org/plosone/article?id=10.1371/journal.pone.0002932. August 13th, 2008.

Ford, James D. "Dangerous Climate Change and the Importance of Adaptation for the Arctic's Inuit Population".
www.earthjustice.org/sites/default/files/black-carbon/ford-et-al-2009-arctic-inuit-adaptation-cc.pdf.
May 28th, 2009.

Ford, James D. Pearce, Tristan. Duerden, Frank. Furgal, Chris. Smit, Barry. "Climate Change Policy Responses for Canada's Inuit Population: The Importance of and Opportunities for Adaptation".
web.law.columbia.edu/sites/default/files/microsites/climate-change/files/Arctic-Resources/Tribal-Organizations/journal%20article%20inuit%20adaptation%20planning.pdf. October 9th, 2009.

OTHER BOOKS FROM EVERGREEN FOREST PUBLISHING

Your Memory Fragments: How to Become the Ideal Person You Imagine

What Your Mom Never Told You About Recessions: 15 Secrets About Recession Investing the Millionaires Are Hiding

ONE LAST THING....

I would like to say a word of thank you for everyone who was able to help me. This book includes several people's recommendations and advices where I was able to summarize it and simplify it for everyone to understand better. I couldn't have done it without those who have helped me. Thank you for everything.

And thank you for purchasing this book. Until next time, this was Benjamin Walters.

THIS IS THE END...

I would like to say thank you for purchasing this book. Without your support, this would have not been possible. So I would like to give you this **free** info graphics that will help you survive recession.

This info graphic will help you be prepared for the most significant financial crisis that everyone struggles from, and instead allow you to earn a massive amount of money during this time of chaos. Did you know there are hundreds of people who became millionaires because they were ready for the recession? Sounds entirely different than everyone else who went through the 2008 recession. But with this info graphics, I assure you that you can be one of those people.

So what are you waiting for? Click on this Link to take advantage of this lifetime opportunity and reach financial freedom.

https://tinyurl.com/recession-infographics

www.ingramcontent.com/pod-product-compliance
Lightning Source LLC
Chambersburg PA
CBHW071044240526
45471CB00014B/564